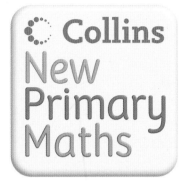

Collins New Primary Maths

Pupil Book 5A

Series Editor: Peter Clarke

Authors: Jeanette Mumford, Sandra Roberts, Andrew Edmondson

Contents

Page number

Get in order!

1 Write out these numbers filling in the missing numbers.

a 4523 4524 ☐ 4526 ☐ 4528 4529 ☐ ☐ 4532

b 6174 ☐ 6176 6177 ☐ ☐ 6180 ☐ 6182 ☐

c 7006 ☐ 7008 ☐ ☐ 7011 ☐ 7013 ☐ ☐

d 9338 ☐ ☐ 9341 ☐ 9343 ☐ ☐ 9346 ☐

e 8299 ☐ 8301 ☐ ☐ 8304 ☐ 8306 ☐ 8308

2 Put each set of numbers in order, from smallest to largest.

a 1862   3496   1748   2956   2832   b 5812   5630   5047   5578   5200
c 6302   6354   3687   3612   3318   d 1985   9143   1830   8144   9102
e What does each red digit in the numbers in d represent?

3 Write one number that comes between these two numbers.

a 1200 ☐ 2310   b 3654 ☐ 4860

c 4002 ☐ 5100   d 5812 ☐ 6584

1 Write the **next** number.

a 12 310 ☐   b 23 540 ☐   c 36 715 ☐

d 45 126 ☐   e 17 822 ☐   f 28 207 ☐

g 31 682 ☐   h 46 930 ☐   i 51 602 ☐

2 What does the red digit in the numbers in **1** represent.

3 Put each set of numbers in order from smallest to largest.

a

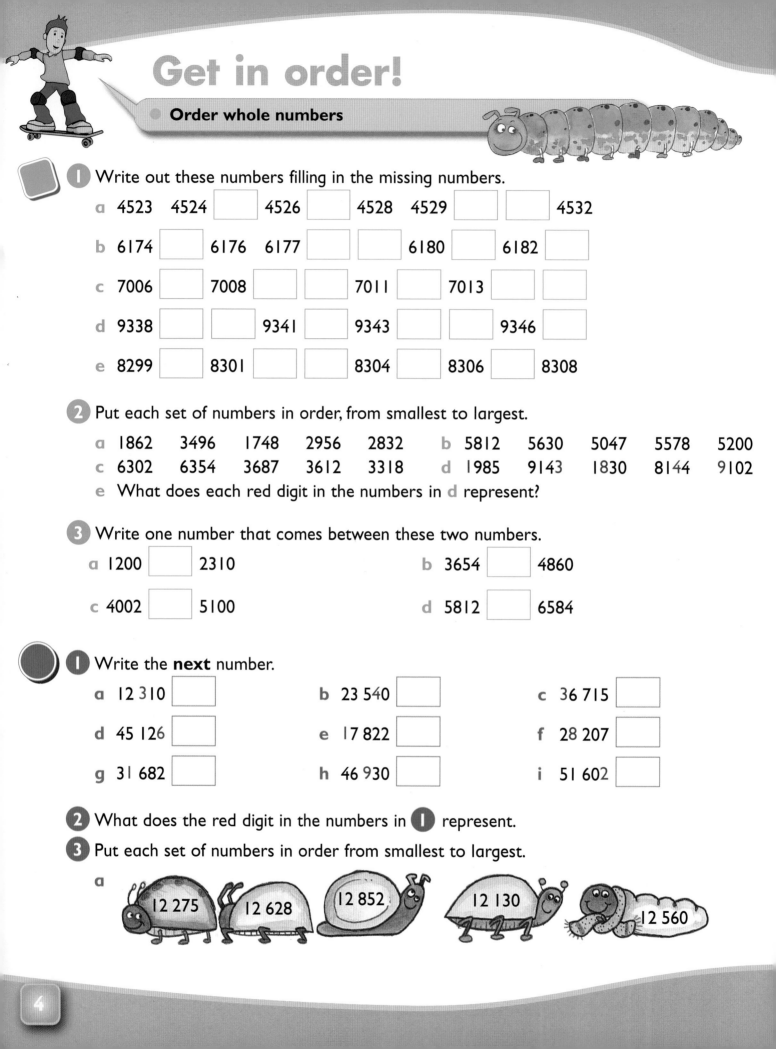

12 275   12 628   12 852   12 130   12 560

4

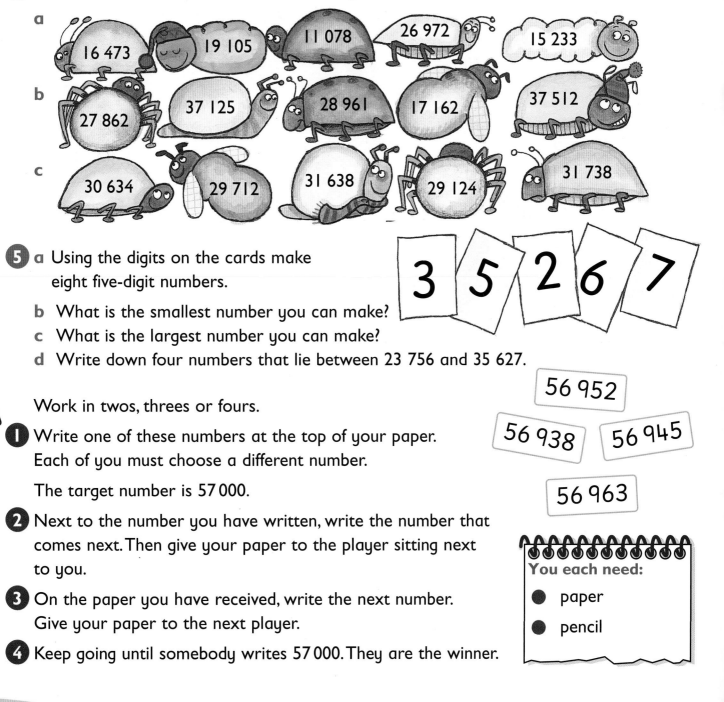

b 17 162   19 324   17 062   18 347   19 836

c 20 628   21 268   28 620   26 806   20 826

4 Put each set of numbers in order from largest to smallest.

a 16 473   19 105   11 078   26 972   15 233

b 27 862   37 125   28 961   17 162   37 512

c 30 634   29 712   31 638   29 124   31 738

5 a Using the digits on the cards make eight five-digit numbers.

3 5 2 6 7

b What is the smallest number you can make?

c What is the largest number you can make?

d Write down four numbers that lie between 23 756 and 35 627.

Work in twos, threes or fours.

1 Write one of these numbers at the top of your paper. Each of you must choose a different number.

The target number is 57 000.

56 952

56 938   56 945

56 963

2 Next to the number you have written, write the number that comes next. Then give your paper to the player sitting next to you.

3 On the paper you have received, write the next number. Give your paper to the next player.

4 Keep going until somebody writes 57 000. They are the winner.

You each need:
● paper
● pencil

Broken bead strings

Order decimals to one place and position them on a number line.

Copy and complete the bead strings.

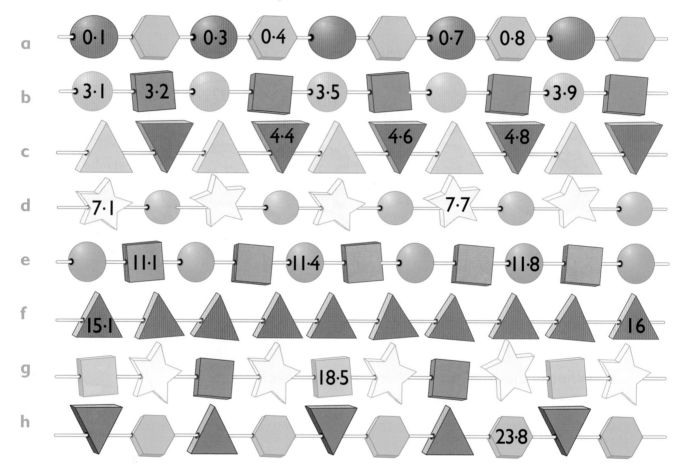

a 0·1 0·3 0·4 0·7 0·8

b 3·1 3·2 3·5 3·9

c 4·4 4·6 4·8

d 7·1 7·7

e 11·1 11·4 11·8

f 15·1 16

g 18·5

h 23·8

Put these bead strings back together in the right order.

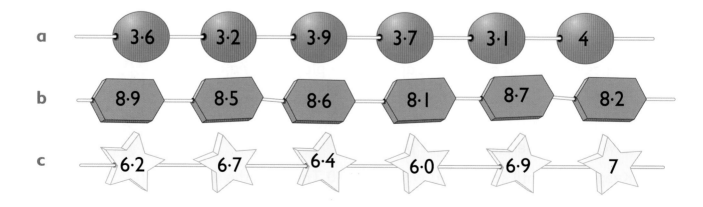

a 3·6 3·2 3·9 3·7 3·1 4

b 8·9 8·5 8·6 8·1 8·7 8·2

c 6·2 6·7 6·4 6·0 6·9 7

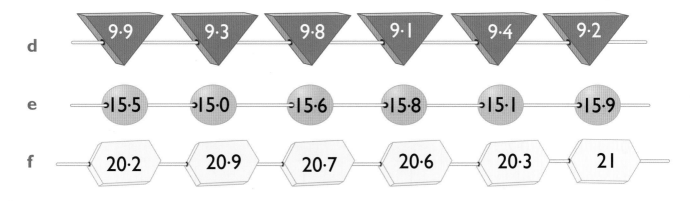

d   9·9 9·3 9·8 9·1 9·4 9·2

e   15·5 15·0 15·6 15·8 15·1 15·9

f   20·2 20·9 20·7 20·6 20·3 21

2 Put these bead strings back together in the right order and fill in the missing numbers.

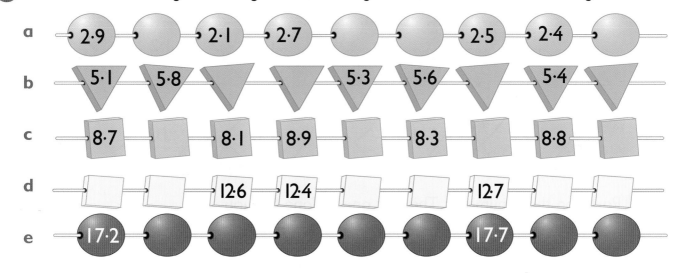

a   2·9 2·1 2·7 2·5 2·4

b   5·1 5·8 5·3 5·6 5·4

c   8·7 8·1 8·9 8·3 8·8

d   12·6 12·4 12·7

e   17·2 17·7

3 Explain how to order numbers to one decimal place if the whole numbers are the same.

  Fractions and decimals go together. Explain how decimals to one place are linked to fractions. Imagine your explanation is for someone who does not understand decimals to one place.

Tent tenths

● **Understand decimal notation for tenths**

1 Write the tenths from 0 to 1 as decimal fractions.

0   0·1   0·2   1

2 Put these decimals in order from smallest to largest. Use the number line to help you.

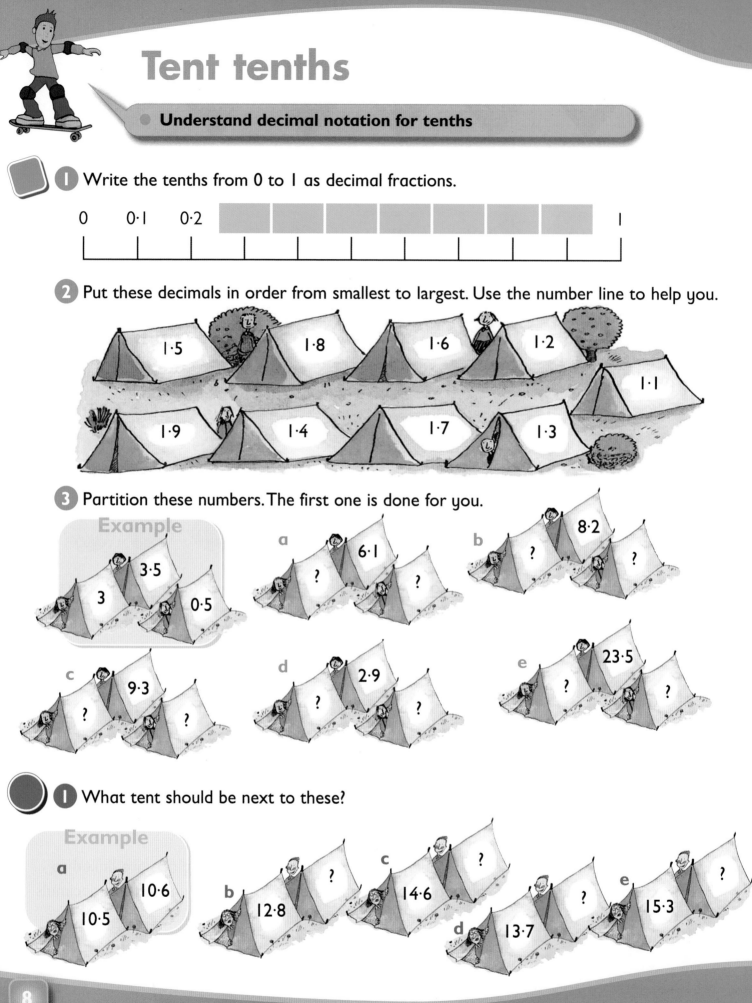

1·5   1·8   1·6   1·2   1·1

1·9   1·4   1·7   1·3

3 Partition these numbers. The first one is done for you.

Example
3·5
3   0·5

a 6·1
?   ?

b 8·2
?   ?

c 9·3
?   ?

d 2·9
?   ?

e 23·5
?   ?

● **1** What tent should be next to these?

Example

a 10·6
10·5

b 12·8   ?

c 14·6   ?

d 13·7   ?

e 15·3   ?

f 17.1 ?
g 16.2 ?
h 11.9 ?
i 16.4 ?
j 19.2 ?

2 What is one tent that will come between these?

Example
a 5.6 5.7 5.9

b 15.2 ? 15.6

c 12.4 ? 12.8

d 21.9 ? 22.5

e 23.4 ? 24.6

f 25.3 ? 23.9

3 Partition these numbers into hundreds, tens, ones and tenths.

a 123.4 ? ? ?

b 156.1 ? ? ?

c 272.9 ? ? ?

d 349.3 ? ? ?

e 442.2 ? ? ?

f 750.7 ? ? ?

1 Use these digits and make 24 two-digit numbers to one decimal place, for example 42.6. Put them in order from smallest to largest.

6 4 2 9

2 Choose two of the numbers. Write all the decimal numbers to one place that lie between them.

Buzzing calculations

Make an addition calculation with each pair of numbers. Work them out mentally. Show your working.

Example

28 + 56 = 84
20 + 50 = 70
8 + 6 = 14

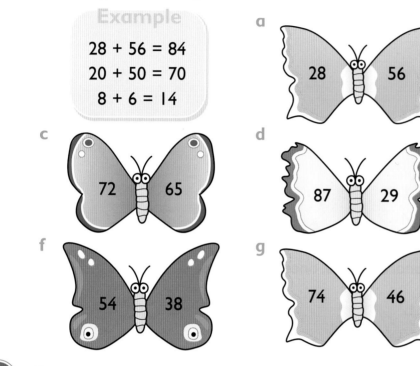

a **28** **56**

b **94** **48**

c **72** **65**

d **87** **29**

e **63** **21**

f **54** **38**

g **74** **46**

h **82** **64**

I Help the bee get back to his hive by working out the calculations on each flower. Choose whether to add them mentally or use a written method.

Remember

Think about the best strategy for each calculation.

a 235 + 401

b 307 + 95

c 97 + 83

d 563 + 248

e 684 + 237

f 93 + 51

You need:
● calculator

10

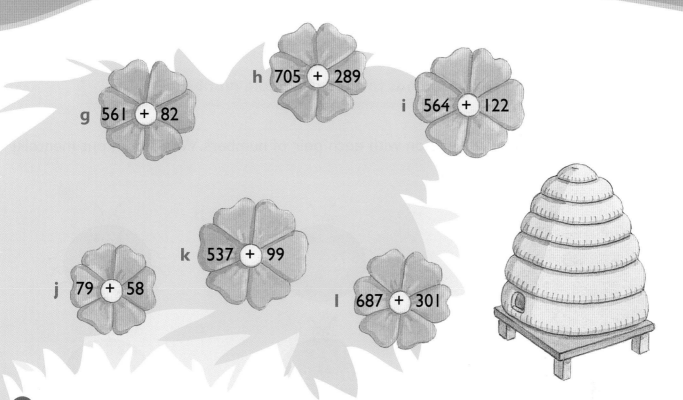

h 705 + 289

g 561 + 82

i 564 + 122

k 537 + 99

j 79 + 58

l 687 + 301

2 Now check your calculations using a calculator. If you got any wrong, work out where you made your mistake.

Work with a partner.
Take turns to write out a vertical addition calculation.

1 One person works it out using the written method.

2 The other person checks the answers using the inverse operation, subtraction, on a calculator.

3 Repeat several times swapping roles.

You need:
● calculator

Example

765 + 896

Creeping calculations

Make a subtraction calculation with each pair of numbers. Work them out mentally. Show your working.

Example

67 − 43 = 24
67 − 40 = 27
27 − 3 = 24

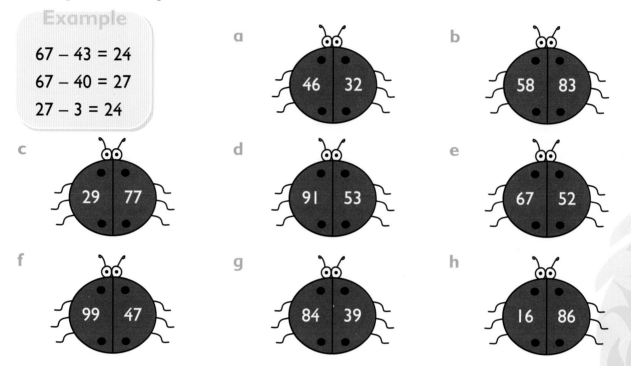

a 46 32

b 58 83

c 29 77

d 91 53

e 67 52

f 99 47

g 84 39

h 16 86

① Help the spider get back to his web by working out the calculations on each flower. Choose whether to subtract using the written method or work it out mentally.

You need:
● calculator

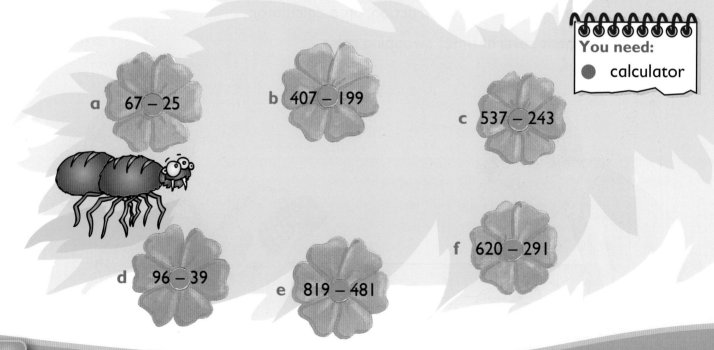

a 67 − 25

b 407 − 199

c 537 − 243

d 96 − 39

e 819 − 481

f 620 − 291

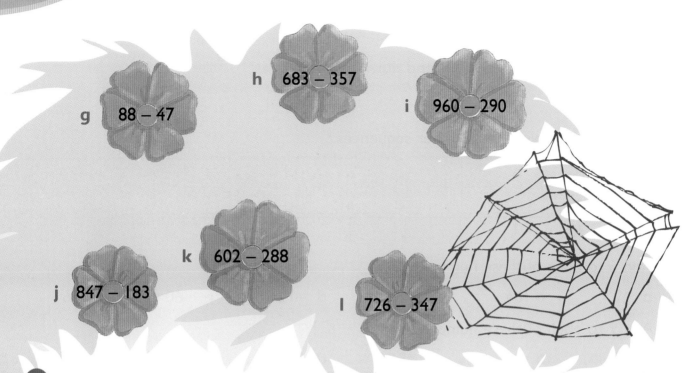

h 683 – 357

g 88 – 47

i 960 – 290

k 602 – 288

j 847 – 183

l 726 – 347

2 Now check your calculations using a calculator. If you got any wrong, work out where you made your mistake.

 Work with a partner.
Take turns to write out a vertical subtraction calculation.

1 One person works it out using the written method.

2 The other person checks the answers using the inverse operation, addition, on a calculator.

3 Repeat several times swapping roles.

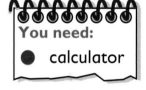
You need:
● calculator

Example

985 – 673

Number sequences

● **Recognise and extend number sequences**

① Copy and complete the number sequences.

a 6, 12, 18, ☐ , ☐ , ☐ , ☐ , ☐ , ☐ , ☐

b 9, 18, 27, ☐ , ☐ , ☐ , ☐ , ☐ , ☐ , ☐

c −36, −30, ☐ , ☐ , ☐ , ☐ , ☐ , ☐ , ☐

② Add 6 to each of these numbers.

a 42   b 64   c 72   d −12   e −60   f 66

③ Add 9 to each of these numbers.

a 27   b −36   c −54   d 99   e 54   f −90

① Copy and complete the number sequences.

a 1, 7, 13, ☐ , ☐ , ☐ , ☐ , ☐ , ☐ , ☐

b 2, 11, 20, ☐ , ☐ , ☐ , ☐ , ☐

c −50, ☐ , ☐ , −23, −14, ☐ , ☐ , ☐

d 60, ☐ , ☐ , ☐ , ☐ , ☐ , 6, −3, −12

e 60, ☐ , ☐ , ☐ , 36, 30, ☐ , ☐

② Find your way back to the spaceship by following the correct sequence on the footprints.

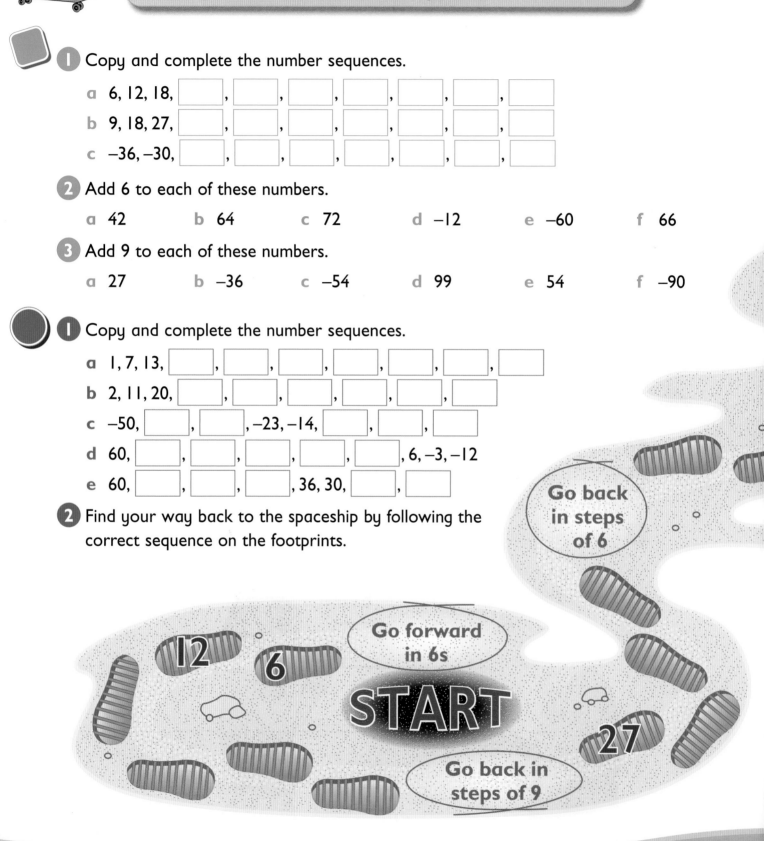

Go back in steps of 6

Go forward in 6s

12

6

START

27

Go back in steps of 9

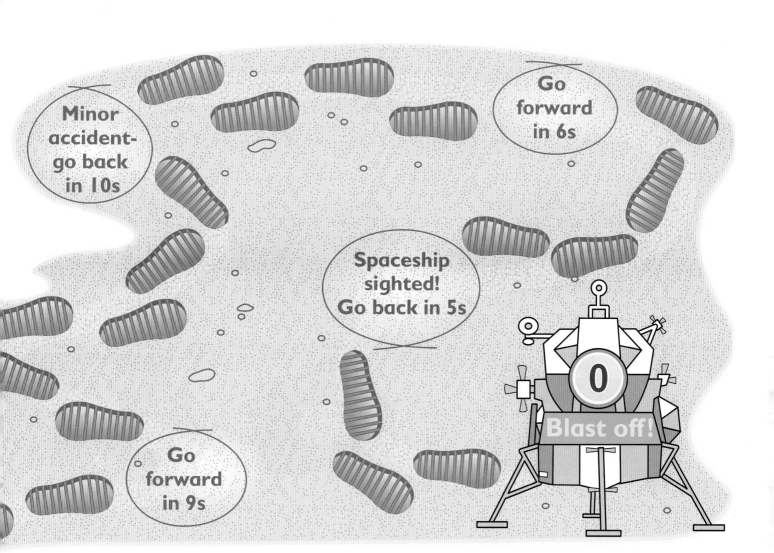

1 Choose a different starting number each time and make 10 jumps.

Jump forwards in:
  a 4s
  b 9s
  c 11s

Jump backwards in:
  d 6s
  e 8s
  f 5s

2 Record each number in sequence.

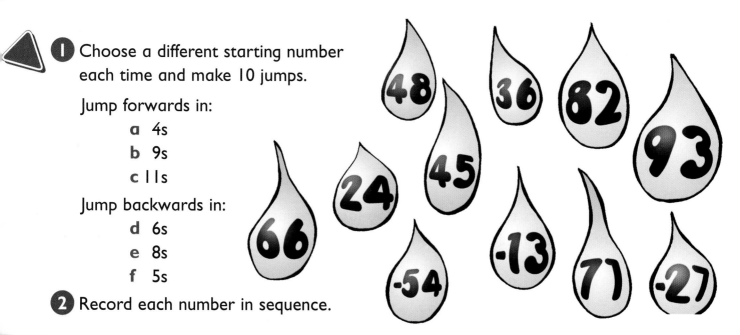

Reviewing multiplication facts

Write a multiplication fact for each number going into the machine. Write the answer.

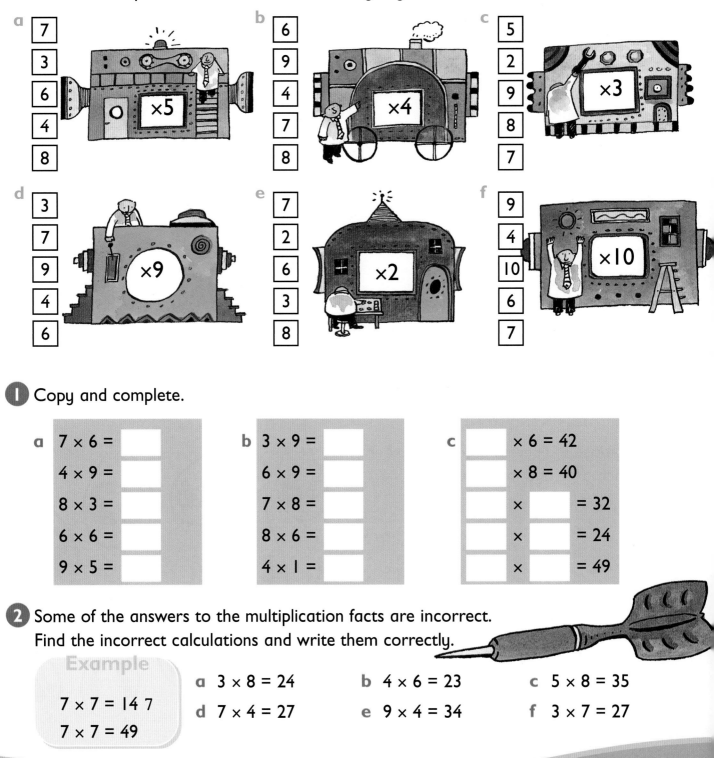

a
7
3
6
4
8

×5

b
6
9
4
7
8

×4

c
5
2
9
8
7

×3

d
3
7
9
4
6

×9

e
7
2
6
3
8

×2

f
9
4
10
6
7

×10

1 Copy and complete.

a 7 × 6 =
4 × 9 =
8 × 3 =
6 × 6 =
9 × 5 =

b 3 × 9 =
6 × 9 =
7 × 8 =
8 × 6 =
4 × 1 =

c ☐ × 6 = 42
☐ × 8 = 40
☐ × ☐ = 32
☐ × ☐ = 24
☐ × ☐ = 49

2 Some of the answers to the multiplication facts are incorrect.
Find the incorrect calculations and write them correctly.

Example

7 × 7 = 14 7
7 × 7 = 49

a 3 × 8 = 24
d 7 × 4 = 27

b 4 × 6 = 23
e 9 × 4 = 34

c 5 × 8 = 35
f 3 × 7 = 27

g 9 × 6 = 56   h 10 × 7 = 70   i 7 × 8 = 57

j 8 × 9 = 72   k 3 × 6 = 15   l 8 × 8 = 62

m 3 × 9 = 29   n 4 × 4 = 12   o 5 × 6 = 30

3 Calculate the score for each dart thrown.

Example

3 × 7 = 21

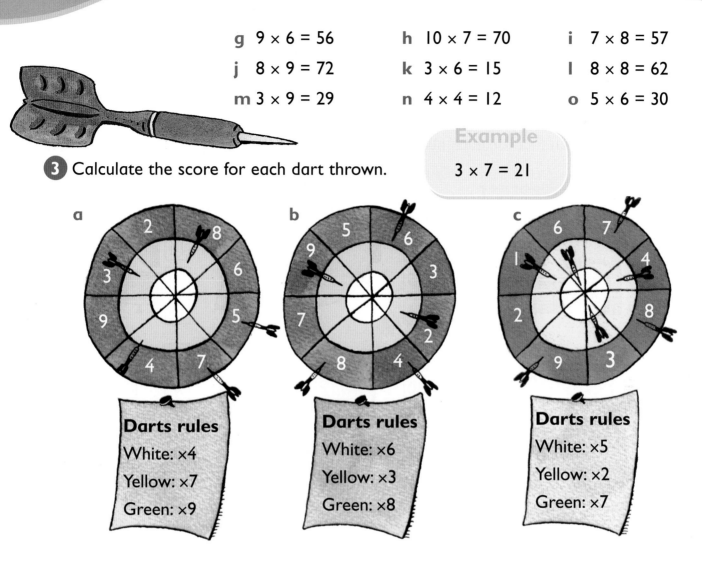

a

Darts rules

White: ×4

Yellow: ×7

Green: ×9

b

Darts rules

White: ×6

Yellow: ×3

Green: ×8

c

Darts rules

White: ×5

Yellow: ×2

Green: ×7

 Copy and complete each of these grids.

Example

3 × 4 = 12

a

×	4	8	1	10
3	12			
8				
6				
9				
5				
1				
7				

b

×		4	2				8
			6	21			
5	45				5	30	
							56

c

×		3		4	
2	12				14
			48	24	
		27			
0					

Reviewing division facts

1 Write a division fact for each number coming out of the machine. Write the answer.

a 24 16 40 32 8 ÷4

b 72 27 63 45 54 ÷9

c 12 18 14 6 16 ÷2

d 35 25 30 40 45 ÷5

e 24 30 27 12 21 ÷3

f 9 4 6 8 7 ÷1

2 Each bowling ball will only hit pins that are multiples of it.
Find the multiples and write a multiplication and division fact for each.

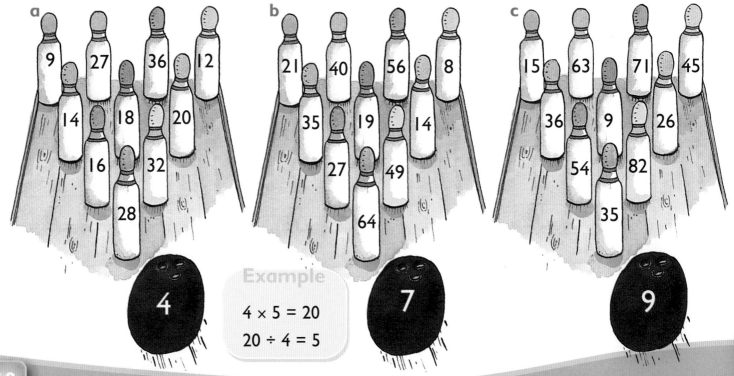

a 9 27 36 12 14 18 20 16 32 28 — ball 4

Example
4 × 5 = 20
20 ÷ 4 = 5

b 21 40 56 8 35 19 14 27 49 64 — ball 7

c 15 63 71 45 36 9 26 54 82 35 — ball 9

18

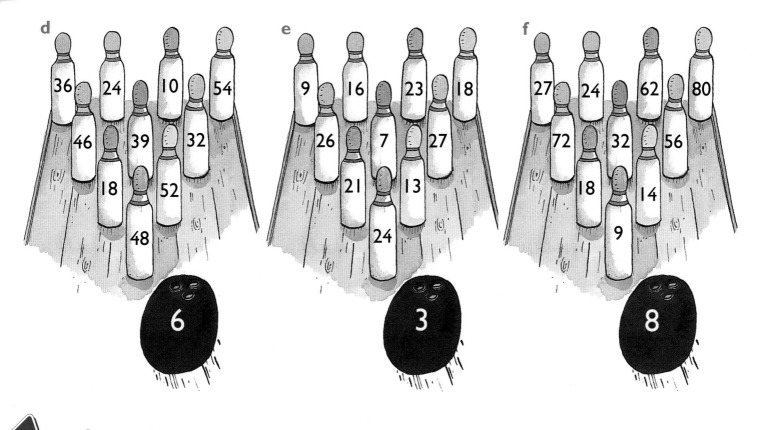

Copy and complete these calculations.

1
a $(32 \div 8) \times 4 = \square$

b $(72 \div 9) \times 3 = \square$

c $(15 \div 3) \times 6 = \square$

d $(27 \div 3) \times 9 = \square$

e $(24 \div 4) \times 7 = \square$

f $(56 \div 7) \times 8 = \square$

g $(36 \div 6) \times 6 = \square$

h $(100 \div 10) \times 0 = \square$

2
a $(32 \div \square) \times 3 = 24$

b $(48 \div \square) \times 5 = 30$

c $(64 \div \square) \times 7 = 56$

d $(12 \div \square) \times 9 = 36$

e $(\square \div 5) \times 6 = 24$

f $(\square \div 3) \times 3 = 21$

g $(\square \div 2) \times 8 = 64$

h $(\square \div 1) \times 9 = 63$

3
a $(35 \div 5) \times \square = 28$

b $(42 \div 6) \times \square = 28$

c $(28 \div 4) \times \square = 28$

d $(63 \div 7) \times \square = 45$

e $(81 \div 9) \times \square = 54$

f $(8 \div 1) \times \square = 56$

g $(49 \div 7) \times \square = 42$

h $(20 \div 5) \times \square = 36$

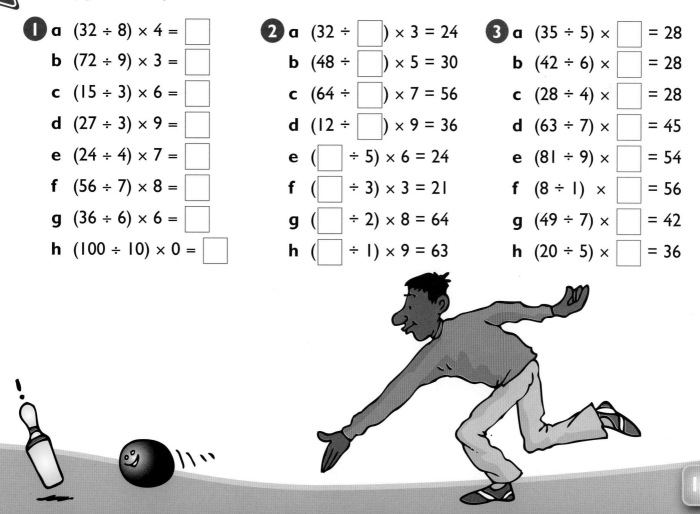

10, 100, 1000

Multiply and divide whole numbers by 10, 100 and 1000

1 Multiply these numbers by 10.

a 7   b 9   c 5   d 29   e 64

f 37   g 56   h 73   i 83   j 152

2 Divide these numbers by 10.

a 80   b 40   c 50   d 320   e 460

f 910   g 570   h 650   i 120   j 3500

1 Multiply these numbers by 10, by 100 and by 1000.
Write your answers as calculations.

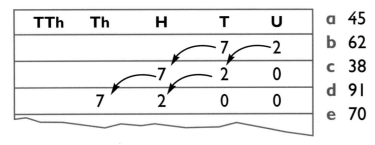

TTh	Th	H	T	U
			7	2
		7	2	0
	7	2	0	0

a 45   f 642
b 62   g 845
c 38   h 963
d 91   i 752
e 70   j 809

k Explain what happens when numbers are multiplied by 10, 100 or 1000.

2 Divide these numbers by 10, by 100 and by 1000.
Write your answers as calculations.

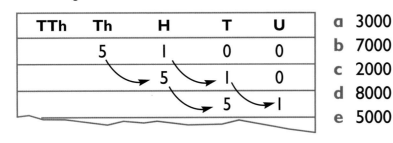

TTh	Th	H	T	U
	5	1	0	0
		5	1	0
			5	1

a 3000   f 84 000
b 7000   g 29 000
c 2000   h 94 000
d 8000   i 61 000
e 5000   j Explain what happens when numbers are divided by 10, 100 or 1000.

3 Each of the following calculations have been either multiplied or divided by 10, 100 or 1000. Copy and complete.

a 700 [   ] = 70

b 550 [   ] = 5500

c 32 [   ] = 3200

d 17 000 [   ] = 17

e 1800 [   ] = 18

f 428 [   ] = 42 800

g 2190 [   ] = 21 900

h 300 [   ] = 3

i 400 [   ] = 400 000

j 5760 [   ] = 576

What to do

Play the game with a partner.

1 Choose a number from the board. Spin the spinner. Carry out the operation on your number and write the answer.

2 Your partner then chooses their number and does the same.

3 The player with the largest answer then covers their chosen number with one of their counters.

4 The winner is the first player to have three counters in a row.

You need:

● 16 counters; 8 of one colour, 8 of another

● paper clip

Each player needs:

● paper and pencil

9100	1700	6300	5600
7600	200	300	2200
4800	500	100	9900
800	8100	7200	1000

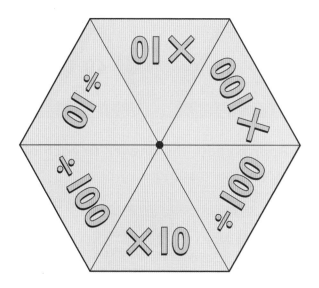

Multiplication

Multiply a two-digit number by a one-digit number

Example

46×7

46×7
$= (40 \times 7) + (6 \times 7)$ or
$= 280 + 42$
$= 322$

Estimate
$50 \times 7 = 350$

	40	6
7	280	42

```
  280
+  42
  322
   ﹍
```
or

```
   46
 ×  7
  280   (40 × 7)
   42   (6 × 7)
  322
   ﹍
```

Copy and complete.

a. 20 ×5 =

b. 40 ×3 =

c. 70 ×9 =

d. 60 ×7 =

e. 50 ×4 =

f. 80 ×7 =

g. 80 ×8 =

h. 30 ×8 =

i. 50 ×3 =

j. 30 ×9 =

k. 80 ×5 =

l. 40 ×7 =

m. 60 ×6 =

n. 90 ×6 =

o. 70 ×4 =

1 Approximate the answer to each of the following. Write the calculation you used to make your estimate.

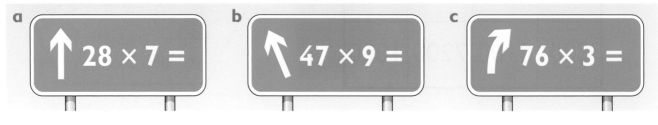

a. 28 × 7 =

b. 47 × 9 =

c. 76 × 3 =

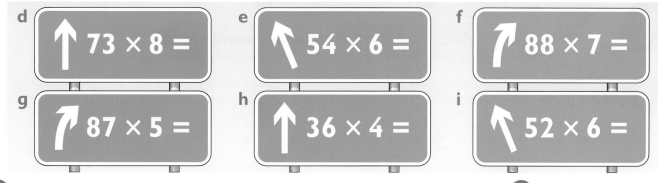

d $73 \times 8 =$

e $54 \times 6 =$

f $88 \times 7 =$

g $87 \times 5 =$

h $36 \times 4 =$

i $52 \times 6 =$

2 Now work out the answer to each of the calculations in question **1**.

3 Arrange each set of 3 digits to make a 2-digit and a 1-digit number. Approximate the answer, then work out the actual answer to each calculation.

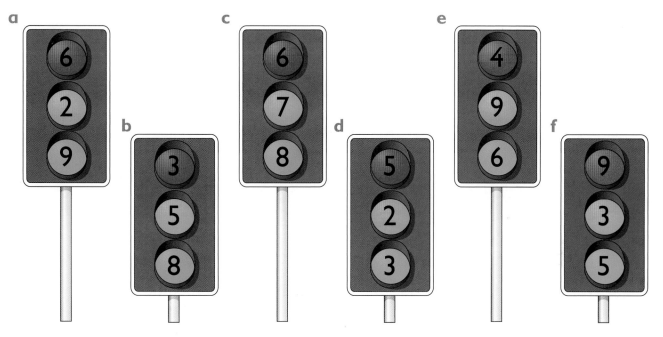

a 6 2 9

b 3 5 8

c 6 7 8

d 5 2 3

e 4 9 6

f 9 3 5

1 Write down any three digits, e.g. 5, 7 and 8, and make a 2-digit number and a 1-digit number.

2 Multiply the two numbers together.

3 By re-arranging the three digits, investigate what other products you can make by multiplying a 2-digit number by a 1-digit number.

4 What is the largest/smallest answer you can make?

Adding, adding, adding

- Use efficient methods to add whole numbers

1 Add these numbers using a mental method. Show your working out for each calculation.

a 67 + 32	b 54 + 21	c 82 + 14	d 63 + 34
e 26 + 51	f 56 + 38	g 29 + 58	h 16 + 74
i 51 + 95	j 79 + 46		

2 Work these calculations out using a standard written method.

a 325 + 432	f 257 + 225
b 783 + 216	g 609 + 373
c 208 + 571	h 476 + 428
d 535 + 243	i 538 + 326
e 619 + 260	j 629 + 346

Be sure to make an estimate first.

1 Add these numbers using a mental method. For the first five calculations record your method as jottings.

a 39 + 61   b 28 + 53   c 64 + 82

d 27 + 94   e 15 + 67   f 46 + 99

g 53 + 87   h 89 + 59   i 77 + 55   j 37 + 94

You need:
● calculator

2 Choose one number from each truck and make up ten addition calculations.

a Estimate the answer.

b Work out the answer using a standard written method.

c Choose two of your calculations and, using jottings, show how you could work them out mentally.

d Now check your calculations using a calculator. If you have made any mistakes work out what you did wrong.

Write out some tips for using the standard written method for addition successfully. Make them helpful for someone who is having problems understanding the method!

Subtracting, subtracting, subtracting

● **Use efficient methods to subtract whole numbers**

1 Subtract these numbers using a mental method. Show your working out for each calculation.

a 54 – 32   b 38 – 21   c 67 – 34   d 83 – 32

e 75 – 43   f 65 – 37   g 82 – 24   h 98 – 86

i 71 – 38   j 82 – 19

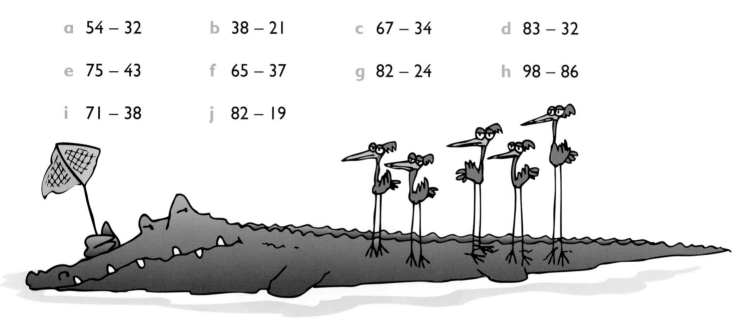

2 Work these calculations out using the standard written method.

a 452 – 231   b 483 – 172   c 675 – 354   d 769 – 505

e 846 – 216   f 541 – 236   g 853 – 325   h 766 – 329

i 674 – 137

Be sure to make an estimate first.

1 Subtract these numbers using a mental method. For the first five calculations record your method as jottings.

You need:
● calculator

a 45 – 19   b 73 – 28   c 67 – 39

d 96 – 24   e 83 – 47   f 88 – 36

g 38 – 14   h 79 – 51   i 69 – 53   j 92 – 86

2 Choose one number from each bus and make up ten subtraction calculations.

a Estimate the answer.

b Work out the answer using a standard written method.

c Choose two of your calculations and, using jottings, show how you could work them out mentally.

d Now check your calculations using a calculator. If you have made any mistakes work out what you did wrong.

Write out some tips for using the standard written method for subtraction successfully. Make them helpful for someone who is having problems understanding the method!

How much?

Add these amounts together using a written method.

a	£6.37	b	£7.76	c	£4.62	d	£3.05	e	£8.72
	+ £5.21		+ £2.19		+ £2.91		+ £6.46		+ £1.34

f	£5.62	g	£16.86	h	£24.36	i	£36.24	j	£42.72
	+ £3.74		+ £21.32		+ £17.21		+ £37.23		+ £33.51

Add these quantities together using a written method.

Remember

The decimal points must go underneath each other.

Example

```
  £36.28
+ £74.53
 £110.81
   ⌐   ⌐
```

a

£36.19 £27.39

b

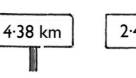

4·38 km   2·47 km

c

29·1 m   86·4 m

d

74·5 kg   42·1 kg

e

£78.65   £15.42

f

97·3 l   40·8 l

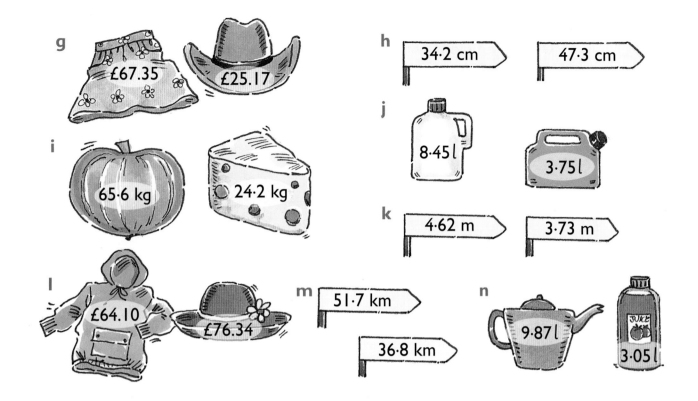

g £67.35 £25.17

h 34·2 cm 47·3 cm

j 8·45 l 3·75 l

i 65·6 kg 24·2 kg

k 4·62 m 3·73 m

l £64.10 £76.34

m 51·7 km 36·8 km

n 9·87 l 3·05 l

How many different totals can you make using these prices?

£78.63

£35.76

£24.38

£52.91

What's the difference?

Subtract these amounts using a written method.

a	£8.72	b	£6.38	c	£5.73	d	£9.74	e	£7.24
	− £6.25		− £3.72		− £2.04		− £6.29		− £3.52

f	£8.36	g	£14.72	h	£25.39	i	£34.62	j	£37.63
	− £4.82		− £12.16		− £17.10		− £22.47		− £19.28

Subtract these quantities from each other to find the difference. Use a written method.

Remember

The decimal points must go underneath each other.

Example

a

£27.62
£15.81

b

6·83 km
4·29 km

c

68·7 m   39·5 m

d

56·5 kg   24·9 kg

e

£25.19
£62.47

f

38·4 l

16·7 l

g £86.28 £21.51

h 47·3 cm 26·5 cm

i 98·2 kg 67·7 kg

j 7·29 l 3·61 l

k 8·91 m 3·56 m

l £72.94 £33.07

m 49·3 km 22·8 km

n 6·50 l 2·43 l

I go shopping with my friend. I start with £98.26. I buy a jacket that costs £23.51.
I buy two tickets for the cinema. They cost £6.70 each. Then I buy lunch and this
costs me £4.81. My friend borrows £45.79 from me to buy some shoes. I see a
great shirt that costs £14.65. Do I have enough money left?
If I do, what will I have left after I buy the shirt? If I don't, how much more
will I need?

Find my numbers

1	2	3	4	~~5~~	6	7	8	9	~~10~~
11	12	13	14	~~15~~	16	17	18	19	~~20~~
21	22	23	24	~~25~~	26	27	28	29	~~30~~
31	32	33	34	~~35~~	36	37	38	39	~~40~~
41	42	43	44	~~45~~	46	47	48	49	~~50~~

You need:
- several 1-50 number grids

Is your number a multiple of five?

No.

A game for 2 players.

1. One player secretly chooses a set of numbers and writes down what this set is.

2. The second player has to ask questions to find out what the set of numbers is. The first player can only answer yes or no.

3. If the first player answers no then they must cross all these numbers out.

4. Keep going until the second player can work out what the set of numbers is.

5. Swap roles.

A game for 2 players.

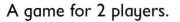

You need:

- several 1-100 number squares

1 One player secretly chooses a set of numbers and writes down what this set is.

2 The second player has to ask questions to find out what the set of numbers is. The first player can only answer yes or no.

3 If the first player answers no then they must cross all these numbers out.

4 Keep going until the second player can work out what the set of numbers is.

5 Swap roles.

1	2	3	4	5	6	7	8	9	10
11	12	13	14	15	16	17	18	19	20
21	22	23	24	25	26	27	28	29	30
31	32	33	34	35	36	37	38	39	40
41	42	43	44	45	46	47	48	49	50
51	52	53	54	55	56	57	58	59	60
61	62	63	64	65	66	67	68	69	70
71	72	73	74	75	76	77	78	79	80
81	82	83	84	85	86	87	88	89	90
91	92	93	94	95	96	97	98	99	100

Is your number a multiple of ten?

No.

Think about the game you have played with your partner. What is the best order to ask your questions to find your partner's numbers in the most efficient way?

Multiplication and division facts

Recall multiplication facts up to 10 x 10 and derive quickly the related division facts

Use each set of cards to make three multiplication facts.

2 7 5

2 × 7 = 14
2 × 5 = 10
7 × 5 = 35

a
5 3 6

b
7 9 6

c
2 4 8

d
9 2 5

e
3 10 8

f
1 5 9

g
10 5 8

h
8 3 9

i
7 6 8

j
4 7 10

k
5 3 4

l
9 4 6

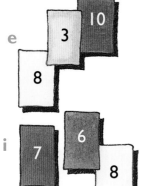
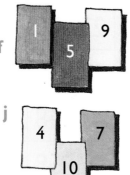
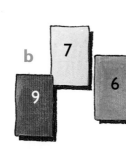

Use the numbers 0 – 10 to find the answers.

a If I multiply the number by 3, the answer is 18.
b If I multiply the number by itself, the answer is 49.
c If I multiply the number by 9, the answer is 72.
d If I multiply the number by 6, the answer is 24.
e Double the number to get an answer of 16.
f Multiply the number by any number to get an answer of 0.

2 Use these number cards and the cards from question **1** to write 20 division calculations.

Example

40 ÷ 4 = 10

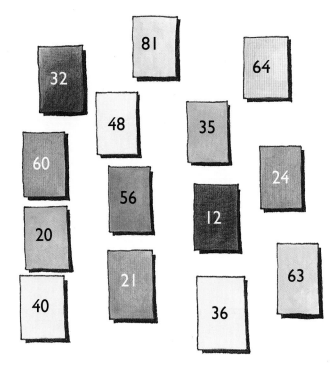

3 Use the words in the boxes and the numbers from questions **1** and **2** to make 20 sentences about numbers. Use each word at least once.

Example

The product of 9 and 3 is 27.

factor

multiplied by

Find 5

A game for 2 players.

1 Take turns to roll the two dice.

2 Multiply the two numbers together.

3 Place a counter over the answer on the number square.

4 The first person to get five counters in a row, horizontal, vertical or diagonal, is the winner.

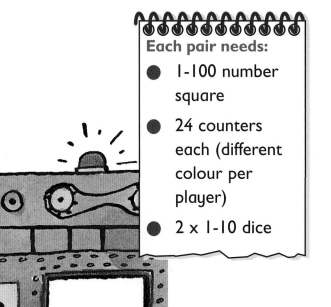

Each pair needs:

● 1-100 number square

● 24 counters each (different colour per player)

● 2 x 1-10 dice

Using multiplication facts

Use multiplication facts to multiply pairs of multiples of 10 and 100

Copy and complete.

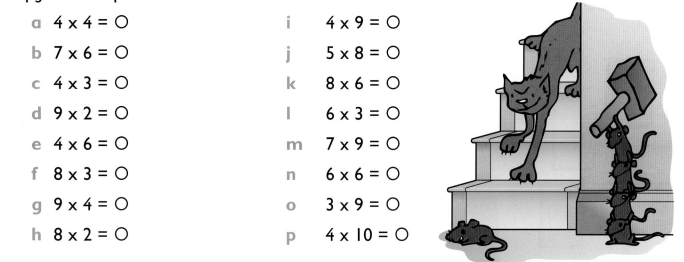

a 4 x 4 = ◯

b 7 x 6 = ◯

c 4 x 3 = ◯

d 9 x 2 = ◯

e 4 x 6 = ◯

f 8 x 3 = ◯

g 9 x 4 = ◯

h 8 x 2 = ◯

i 4 x 9 = ◯

j 5 x 8 = ◯

k 8 x 6 = ◯

l 6 x 3 = ◯

m 7 x 9 = ◯

n 6 x 6 = ◯

o 3 x 9 = ◯

p 4 x 10 = ◯

1 Copy and complete each set of calculations.

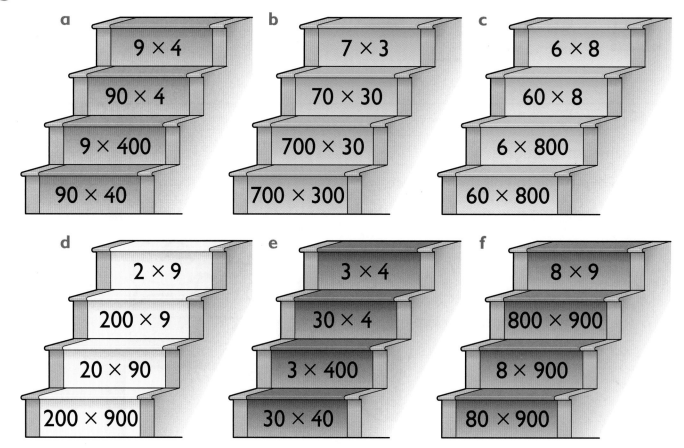

a
9×4
90×4
9×400
90×40

b
7×3
70×30
700×30
700×300

c
6×8
60×8
6×800
60×800

d
2×9
200×9
20×90
200×900

e
3×4
30×4
3×400
30×40

f
8×9
800×900
8×900
80×900

2 Use your knowledge of the times tables facts up to 10 x 10 to help you work out the answers to these calculations.

a 50 x 4 = ○

b 7 x 30 = ○

c 700 x 3 = ○

d 90 x 40 = ○

e 9 x 600 = ○

f 20 x 50 = ○

g 300 x 80 = ○

h 600 x 2 = ○

i 800 x 300 = ○

j 60 x 6 = ○

k 3 x 90 = ○

l 500 x 70 = ○

m 80 x 90 = ○

n 3 x 600 = ○

o 700 x 900 = ○

p 600 x 10 = ○

1 Copy and complete.

a 70 x ○ = 4900

b ○ x 80 = 3200

c 30 x ○ = 180

d 40 x ○ = 20 000

e ○ x 600 = 420 000

f ○ x 900 = 2700

g ○ x 700 = 56 000

h 300 x ○ = 18 000

i 90 x ○ = 1800

j ○ x 40 = 2800

2

I know that 8 x 6 = 48.
I used this to work out
that 80 x 6 = 480.

Write 10 other multiplication
or division facts that are related
to 8 x 6 = 48.

Finding factors

Find all the pairs of factors of any number up to 100

1. How many different ways can you divide 24 pegs to make a rectangular shape?
Write a multiplication fact for each shape you make.

Example

$4 \times 6 = 24$

You need:
- a pegboard and pegs

2. Use the number of pegs shown to make square or rectangular shapes. Write a multiplication fact for each shape made.

a   16 pegs
b   20 pegs
c   32 pegs

d   36 pegs
e   18 pegs
f   40 pegs

1. Fill in the missing **factors**.
Copy and complete.

a
$\square \times 5 = 25$
$\square \times 3 = 18$
$4 \times \square = 24$
$10 \times \square = 70$
$\square \times 6 = 30$

b
$\square \times 2 = 18$
$\square \times 7 = 21$
$7 \times \square = 35$
$4 \times \square = 32$
$\square \times \square = 12$

2. Fill in the missing **products**.
Copy and complete.

a
$7 \times 4 = \square$
$6 \times 6 = \square$
$3 \times 9 = \square$
$8 \times 5 = \square$
$9 \times 6 = \square$

b
$4 \times 4 = \square$
$9 \times 3 = \square$
$6 \times 8 = \square$
$7 \times 7 = \square$
$8 \times 4 = \square$

3. Write two multiplication number sentences for each set of numbers. Decide which numbers are the factors and which number is the product.

a   7   3   21
b   7   42
c   8   6   64
d   8   9   36   4

Example

$3 \times 6 = 18$
$6 \times 3 = 18$
Factors = 3 and 6
Product = 18

(3, 6, 18)

38

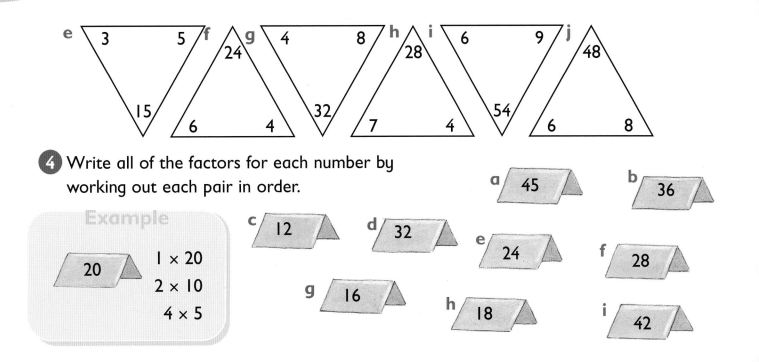

e. 3, 5, 15
f. 24, 6
g. 4, 8, 4
h. 28, 32, 7
i. 6, 4
j. 9, 48, 54, 6, 8

4 Write all of the factors for each number by working out each pair in order.

Example

20 — 1 × 20 / 2 × 10 / 4 × 5

a. 45
b. 36
c. 12
d. 32
e. 24
f. 28
g. 16
h. 18
i. 42

Find the factor

A game for 3–4 players.

- Spread out the two sets of 1–10 number cards face down on the table.

- Shuffle the other number cards and place them face down in one pile on the table.

- Take turns to select a number card from the pile.

- Turn over one card from the table. If it is a factor, keep the card and select another card from the pile.

- If it is not a factor, replace the card face down on the table.

- The player with the most cards at the end is the winner.

Your group needs:

- 2 sets of 1–10 number cards

- Number cards 12, 14, 15, 16, 18, 20, 21, 24, 25, 27, 30, 32, 36, 40, 42

39

Multiples and common multiples

Using a 1-100 number square, circle (○) all the multiples of 6 and draw a cross (✗) through all the multiples of 7.

Which numbers have you circled and drawn a cross through?

Describe what these numbers are.

1	2	3	4	5	⑥	✗	8	9	10
11	12	13	14	15	16	17	18	19	20
21	22	23	24	25	26	27	28	29	30
31	32	33	34	35	36	37	38	39	40
41	42	43	44	45	46	47	48	49	50
51	52	53	54	55	56	57	58	59	60
61	62	63	64	65	66	67	68	69	70
71	72	73	74	75	76	77	78	79	80
81	82	83	84	85	86	87	88	89	90
91	92	93	94	95	96	97	98	99	100

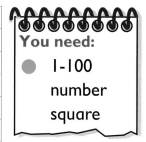

You need:
● 1-100 number square

① Copy and complete the first ten multiples of each sequence.

6		18							
7			28						
8				40					
9									90

Example
$2 \times 6 = 12$

② The numbers have escaped! Find the multiples of 6, 7, 8 and 9. Write a multiplication fact for each multiple you find.

3 Find all the two-digit common multiples of:

a 5 and 7   b 3 and 6   c 4 and 10
d 2 and 9   e 8 and 7   f 3 and 4

Find your way through the obstacle course by following the correct sequence. Start by going up in 6s.

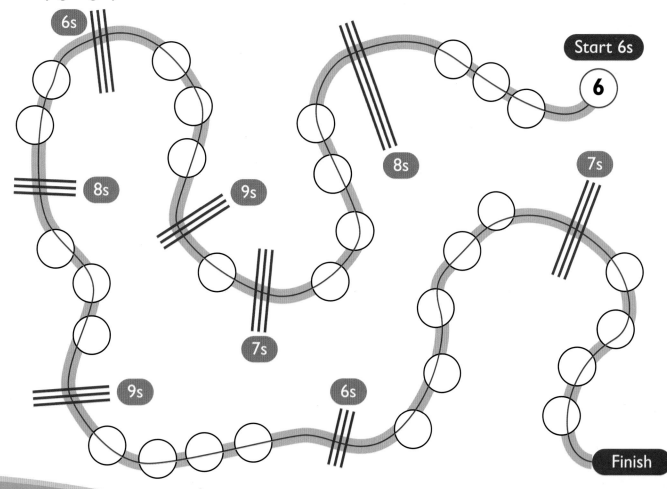

More multiples and common multiples

Using a 1-100 number square, circle (O) all the multiples of 8 and draw a cross (X) through all the multiples of 9.

Which numbers have you circled and drawn a cross through?

Describe what these numbers are.

1	2	3	4	5	6	7	8	9	10
11	12	13	14	15	16	17	18	19	20
21	22	23	24	25	26	27	28	29	30
31	32	33	34	35	36	37	38	39	40
41	42	43	44	45	46	47	48	49	50
51	52	53	54	55	56	57	58	59	60
61	62	63	64	65	66	67	68	69	70
71	72	73	74	75	76	77	78	79	80
81	82	83	84	85	86	87	88	89	90
91	92	93	94	95	96	97	98	99	100

You need:
- 1-100 number square

Draw your own Venn diagrams like the ones below.
Sort the numbers 1 to 90 to match the labels.
Write any numbers that belong in both sets in the (middle) intersecting set.

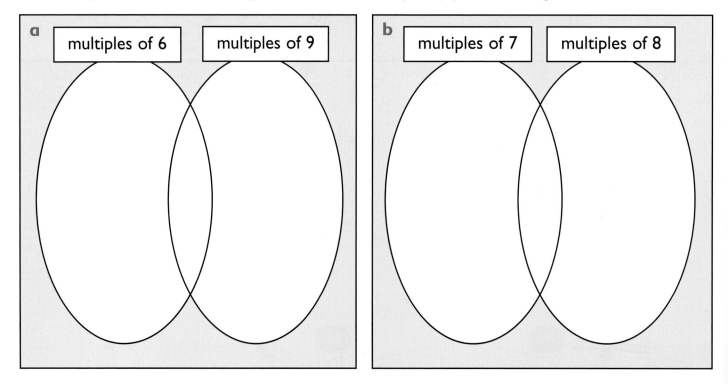

a multiples of 6   multiples of 9

b multiples of 7   multiples of 8

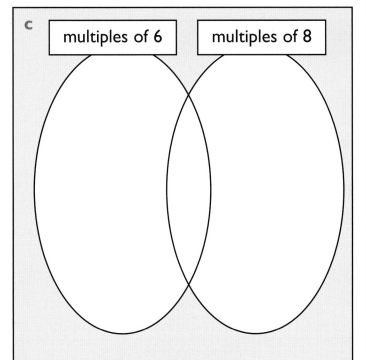

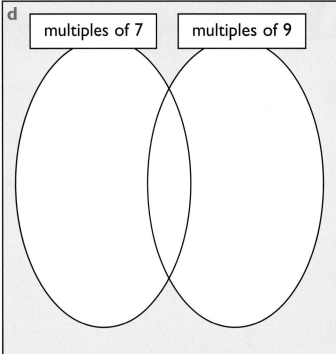

Multiple snap

A game for 2-3 players.

1 Before the game, choose a number between 2 and 10, e.g. 6. The aim of the game is to find all the multiples of the number.

2 Shuffle the number cards and divide them evenly between the players.

3 Each player places their cards in a pile, face down on the table.

4 Players take turns to select the top card one at a time and place it face up on to the centre pile.

Your group needs:
- 1-100 number cards

5 If the top card is a multiple of 6, the first player to identify and touch the pile calling out 'Snap!' collects the pile of cards and adds these to the bottom of their existing pile.

6 The game continues until one player has all of the number cards.

Variation

Use a different number; choose multiples of 7, 8 or 9.

Solid sorts

Look at the 8 shapes in the ● activity.
Copy and complete the Carroll diagram.
Write the name of the shape in the correct region.

Number of edges meeting at a vertex

	3	more than 3
Has at least 1 right-angled face		
Has no right-angled faces		

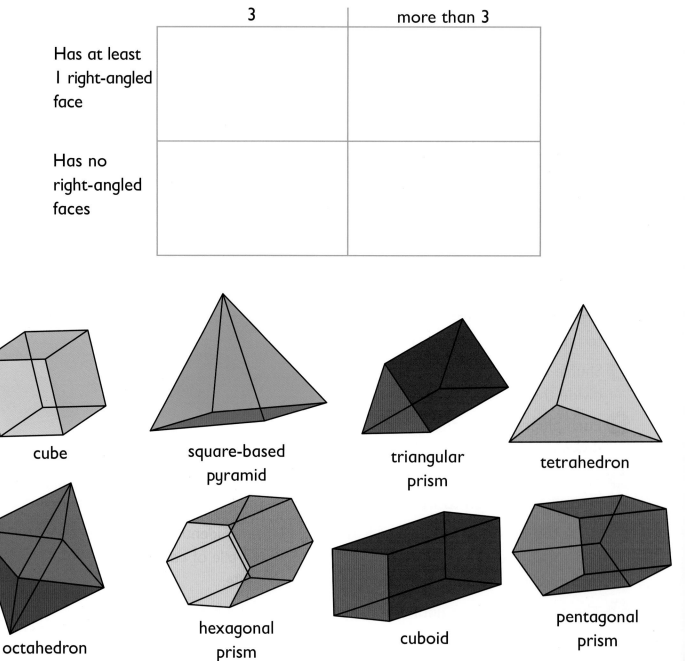

cube

square-based pyramid

triangular prism

tetrahedron

octahedron

hexagonal prism

cuboid

pentagonal prism

1 Copy and complete the Venn diagrams. Write the name of the shape in the correct region.

a cuboid, octahedron, cube, triangular prism

b tetrahedron, square-based pyramid, hexagonal prism, pentagonal prism

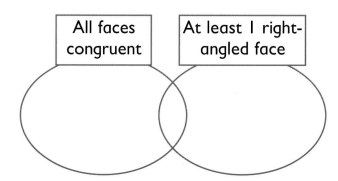

All faces congruent | At least 1 right-angled face

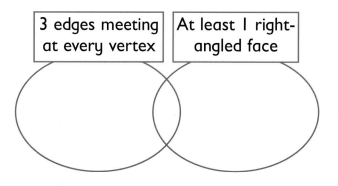

3 edges meeting at every vertex | At least 1 right-angled face

2 For each clue, choose from the 8 solids shown above.
Find and write the name of the solid which has:

a 8 vertices and all right-angled faces congruent to each other.

b 4 edges meeting at every vertex and all faces are triangular.

c the same number of right-angled vertices as a cube, but edges of different lengths.

d 4 more vertices than a cube and the 2 identical end faces are regular.

e one right-angled face and 4 edges meeting at one of the vertices.

3 Write your own clues for these solids.

a tetrahedron   **b** hexagonal prism

In the 18th century a Swiss mathematician, Leonard Euler (pronounced Oiler) said:

'The sum of the number of faces and vertices is always equal to the number of edges plus two.'

1 Is Euler's claim true or false?
Copy and complete this table for each of the 8 shapes on the opposite page.

Name of solid	Faces	Vertices	Edges
cube	6	8	12

2 Does Euler's rule, $F + V = E + 2$, work for a cone?

Visualising 3-D solids

Visualise 3-D solids from 2-D drawings

1. Make each of these shapes, in turn, with interlocking cubes of the same colour.

2. Work out the least number of cubes needed to turn each shape into a cuboid or cube.

3. Now add that amount of cubes, in the second colour, to the shape to check that you are correct.

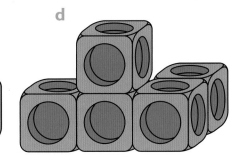

You need:

- about 12 interlocking cubes in two colours

a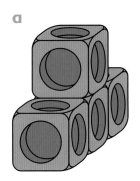

b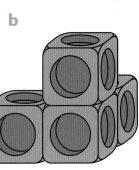

c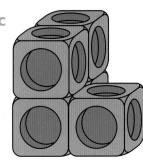

d

1. Work out the least number of interlocking cubes you need to turn each shape into a cuboid.

You need:

- about 12 interlocking cubes in two colours

a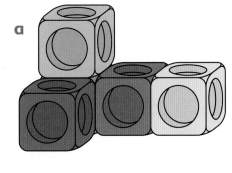

b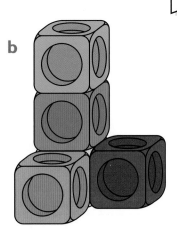

c

2. Simon is stacking shelves in a supermarket.
He fills the spaces on the shelves and makes a cuboid display of each type of packet.
The diagrams show how many packets are on each shelf.

Work out the least number of cartons Simon must add to make each display a cuboid.

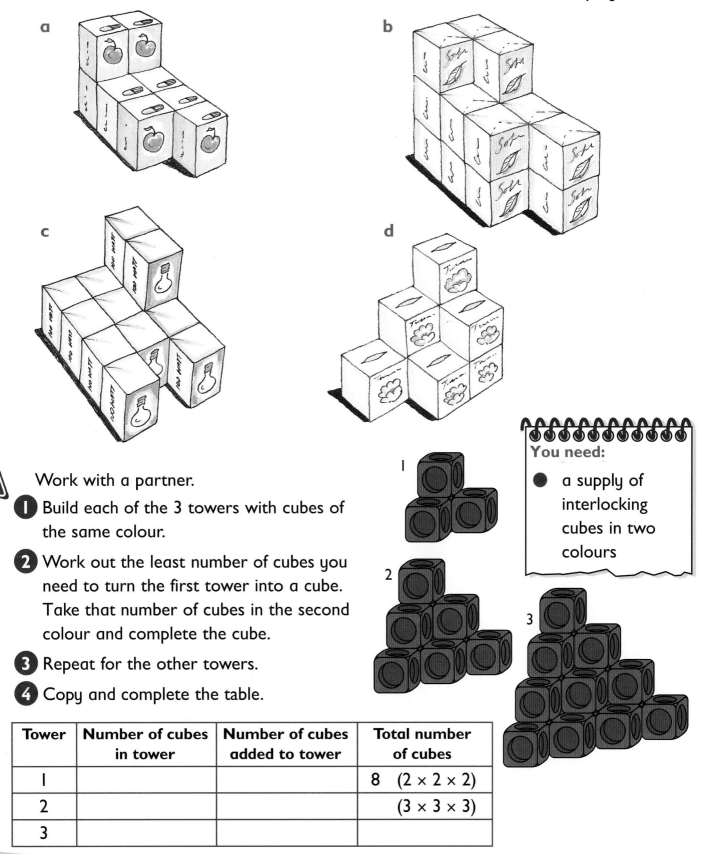

a

b

c

d

Work with a partner.

1 Build each of the 3 towers with cubes of the same colour.

2 Work out the least number of cubes you need to turn the first tower into a cube. Take that number of cubes in the second colour and complete the cube.

3 Repeat for the other towers.

4 Copy and complete the table.

1

2

3

You need:

● a supply of interlocking cubes in two colours

Tower	Number of cubes in tower	Number of cubes added to tower	Total number of cubes
1			8 (2 × 2 × 2)
2			(3 × 3 × 3)
3			

Nets of open cubes

There is a different design on each face of an open cube.

Here are four views of the open cube.

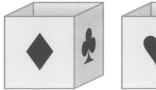

You need:
● 1 cm squared paper
● ruler

Copy the net and draw the faces in the correct place to make the open cube.

1. Some of these shapes are nets of an open cube.
   Make each shape with your interlocking square tiles, then fold it up.

2. Copy and complete the table.
   Mark with a ✓ if the shape is a net of an open cube.
   Mark with a ✗ if the shape is not.

You need:
● 5 interlocking square tiles

Shape	Is a net	Is not a net
a	✓	
b		
c		

a

b

c

d

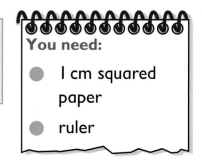

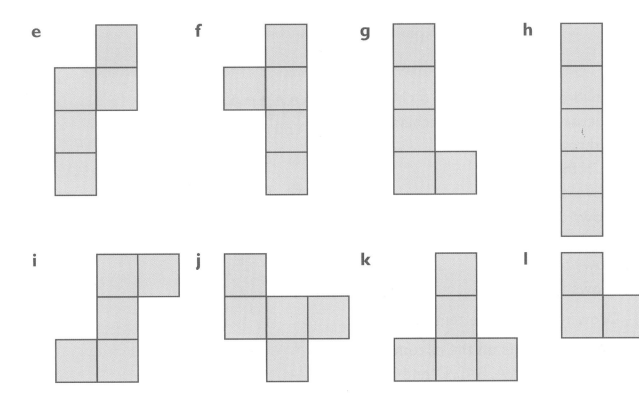

e f g h

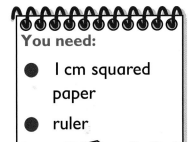

i j k l

Copy these nets on to 1 cm squared paper. For each set of four nets, find a different way to add one square and turn the net for an open cube into the net for a closed cube.

HINT

The bottom face is shaded.

You need:

● 1 cm squared paper

● ruler

a

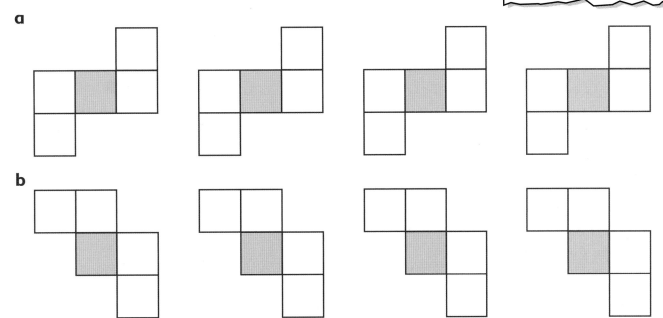

b

Diagonal lines

Recognise and explain patterns and relationships in 2-D shapes

Five children are standing in a circle to practise throwing and catching a ball. They throw the ball to each other in this order.

A throws to C
C throws to E
E throws to B
B throws to D
D throws to A

Remember

Use a ruler.

a Draw round a circle template.

b Mark five points on the circumference and label them A, B, C, D and E.

c Draw straight lines to show the throws the children made.

d Next, join the points in order: A to B to C to D to E to A.

e Name the shape you have made.

1 a Copy these diagonals on to square dot paper.

b Join the vertices in order to complete each shape.

c Find the matching shape above and write its letter.

Remember

Use a ruler.

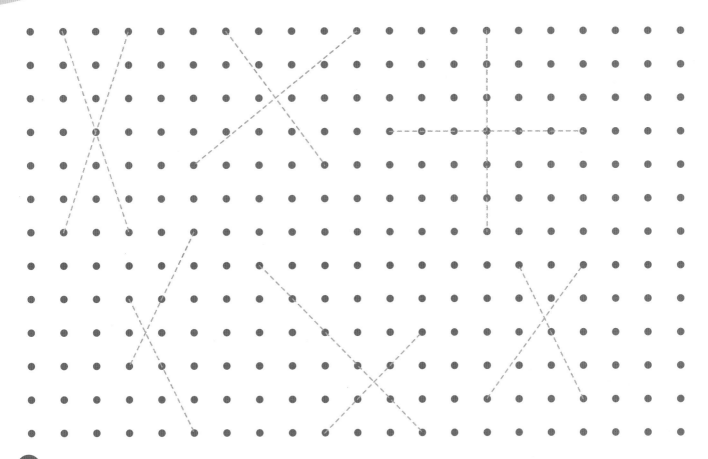

2 **a** Copy these pentagons and hexagons.

b Draw all the diagonals for each shape.

c Draw two more concave pentagons and two more concave hexagons.

d Count the diagonals in each polygon and write what you notice.

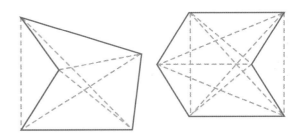

1 How many diagonals can you draw, without them crossing each other, in

a a quadrilateral

b a pentagon

c a hexagon

d a heptagon

e an octagon?

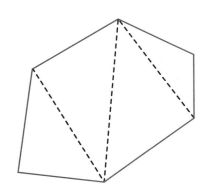

2 Make a table of your results and write about any patterns you notice.

3 What if you had a nine-sided shape? Can you predict the number of diagonals there will be which do not cross each other?

All about rectangles

1 Draw these diagonals on 1 cm squared paper.

2 Use a ruler to draw the four sides of the quadrilateral.

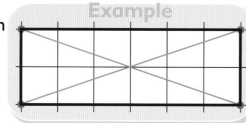

Example

You need:

● 1 cm squared paper

● ruler

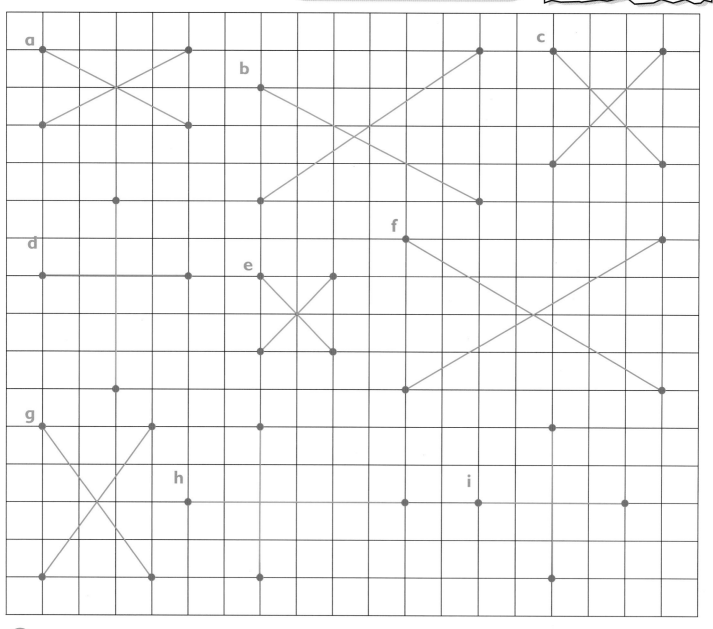

3 Write the letter of the quadrilaterals which are:

a rectangles

b squares

The end branches of this decision tree show the sorting of some triangles and quadrilaterals.

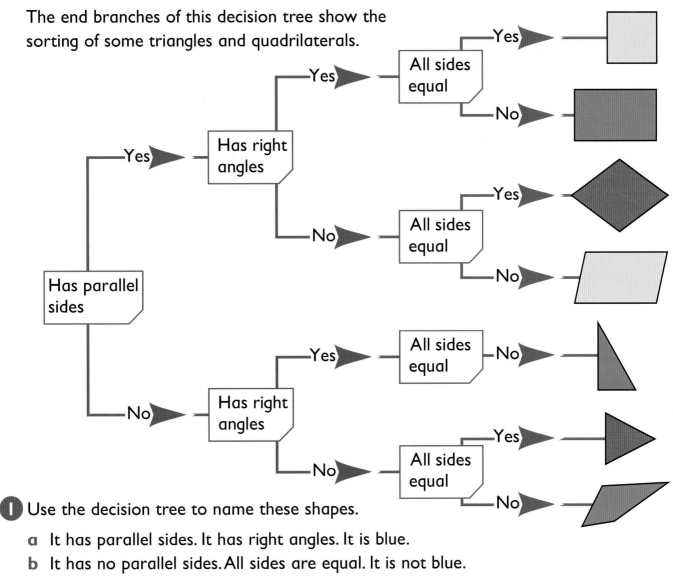

1 Use the decision tree to name these shapes.

a It has parallel sides. It has right angles. It is blue.

b It has no parallel sides. All sides are equal. It is not blue.

c It has parallel sides, right angles and all sides are equal.

d It has no parallel sides. It has a right angle. It is blue.

2 Write a description for these shapes.

a   b

3 On which branch will these shapes finish?

a   b

Statement: *Only in quadrilaterals which are rectangles will the second diagonal bisect the first diagonal into two equal parts.*

True or false? Investigate.

Kilometres to millimetres

● **Convert units of length using decimals**

1 Copy and complete.

a 1 km = 1000 m

$\frac{1}{2}$ km =

$\frac{1}{4}$ km =

$\frac{1}{10}$ km =

$\frac{7}{10}$ km =

$1\frac{3}{4}$ km =

b 1 m = 100 cm

$\frac{1}{2}$ m =

$\frac{1}{4}$ m =

$\frac{1}{10}$ m =

$\frac{7}{10}$ m =

$1\frac{3}{4}$ m =

c 1 cm = 10 mm

$\frac{1}{2}$ cm =

$\frac{1}{4}$ cm =

$\frac{1}{10}$ cm =

$\frac{7}{10}$ cm =

$1\frac{3}{4}$ cm =

> **Example**
>
> $4\frac{1}{4}$ km = 4250 m

2 Write each set of lengths in order, starting with the longest.

a 3100 m, 3·5 km, $3\frac{1}{4}$ km, 3·45 km

b 600 m, 0·7 km, $\frac{3}{4}$ km, 6000 m

c 4·25 m, 500 cm, $4\frac{1}{2}$ m, $4\frac{9}{10}$ m

d 20 mm, 2·1 cm, 180 mm, 19 cm

1 Write in metres how far each hiker walked.

a 8·5 km

b 7·235 km

c 9·06 km

d $10\frac{3}{4}$ km

e $14\frac{3}{10}$ km

f 12·045 km

> **Example**
>
> 4·25 km = 4250 m

2 Write in kilometres the distance on each signpost.

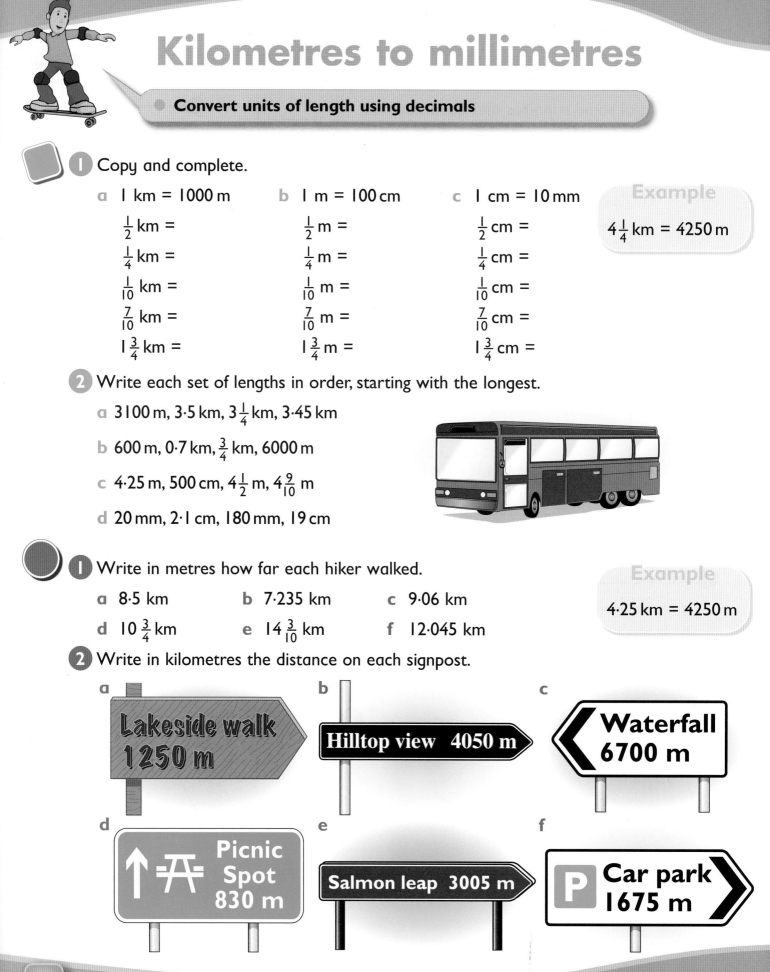

a Lakeside walk 1250 m

b Hilltop view 4050 m

c Waterfall 6700 m

d Picnic Spot 830 m

e Salmon leap 3005 m

f P Car park 1675 m

3 Write each height in centimetres.

a bridge b fence c wall d bluebell e mountain
$3\frac{3}{4}$ m 0·95 m 1·375 m 138 mm 0·864 km

4 The table shows how far each hiker walked in 1 hour.

Hiker	Andy	Benji	Cara	Dean	Emma	Freya
Distance	5·79 km	$5\frac{1}{4}$ km	$5\frac{6}{10}$ km	5840 m	5·7 km	5·085 km

a Who walked the furthest in 1 hour?

b How many metres separated the first and last hiker?

c How many metres was Andy ahead of Freya?

Two climbers reach the cairn at the top of Ben Muckle.

One climber records the height of the mountain in her log book and then adds a few lines.

```
   791
 - 197
   594
 + 495
  1089
```

Lisa said, 'I can make all the mountain tops we can see the same height.'

'Nonsense,' said her friend.

Is Lisa correct? Investigate for these mountains.

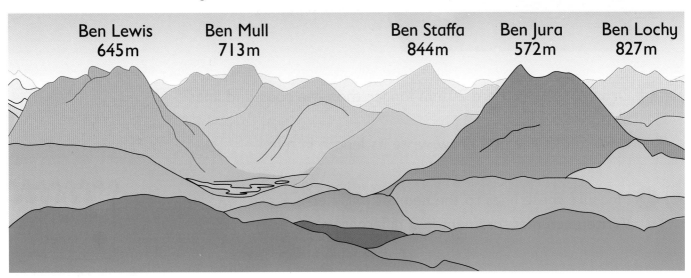

Ben Lewis 645 m
Ben Mull 713 m
Ben Staffa 844 m
Ben Jura 572 m
Ben Lochy 827 m

Measuring in millimetres

Measure and draw lines to the nearest millimetre

1 Measure these rods and lines to the nearest millimetre.
   Write your measurements in 3 different ways.

You need:
● ruler

2 Draw lines which are 20 mm longer than the rods and lines
   in 1 a to f.
   Under each line you draw, write its length in mm.

1 Measure these lines to the nearest millimetre.
   Write each measurement in 3 different ways.

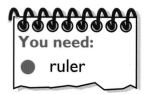

You need:
● ruler

Example

42 mm = 4 cm 2 mm = 4 · 2 cm

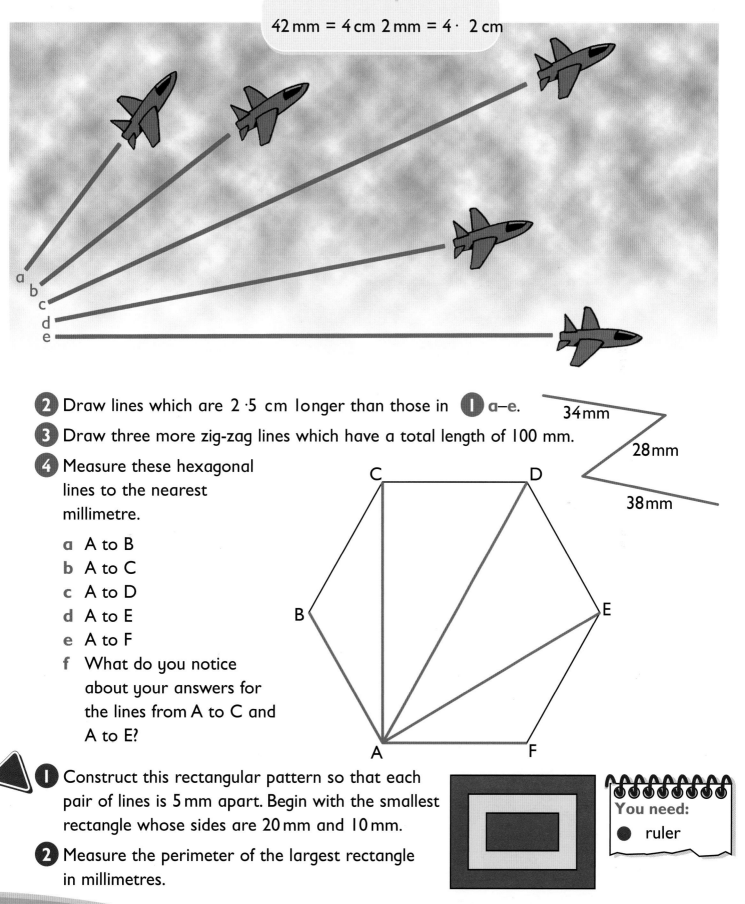

a
b
c
d
e

2 Draw lines which are 2·5 cm longer than those in **1** a–e.

34 mm

3 Draw three more zig-zag lines which have a total length of 100 mm.

28 mm

4 Measure these hexagonal lines to the nearest millimetre.

38 mm

C   D

B   E

a A to B

b A to C

c A to D

d A to E

e A to F

f What do you notice about your answers for the lines from A to C and A to E?

A   F

1 Construct this rectangular pattern so that each pair of lines is 5 mm apart. Begin with the smallest rectangle whose sides are 20 mm and 10 mm.

You need:
● ruler

2 Measure the perimeter of the largest rectangle in millimetres.

DIY measurements

- Convert larger to smaller units (e.g. m to cm or mm)
- Choose and use appropriate operations to solve simple word problems

1 Copy and complete these arrow diagrams. The first one is done for you.

is the same length as
⟷

5 m ⟷ 500 cm   5 m ⟷ 5000 mm

2 m ⟷ [ ] cm   2 m ⟷ [ ] mm

0·5 m ⟷ [ ] cm   [ ] m ⟷ 500 mm

[ ] m ⟷ 20 cm   0·2 m ⟷ [ ] mm

2

400 mm

is the same length as
⟷

40 cm ⟷ 0·4 m

Draw and complete the 3-way relationship for each of the following.

a   40 cm   b   500 mm   c   0·6 m
d   25 cm   e   900 mm   f   0·8 m

1 Write these heights in metres.

a   420 cm   b   800 cm   c   750 cm
d   1500 cm   e   3800 cm   f   6900 cm

Example
730 cm = 7·3 m

2 Write these lengths in millimetres.

a $\frac{1}{10}$ m   b $\frac{3}{10}$ m   c $\frac{7}{10}$ m
d   0·5 m   e   0·1 m   f   0·6 m

Example
$\frac{1}{10}$ m = 100 mm

3 Tiles are measured in millimetres.
Write these dimensions in centimetres.

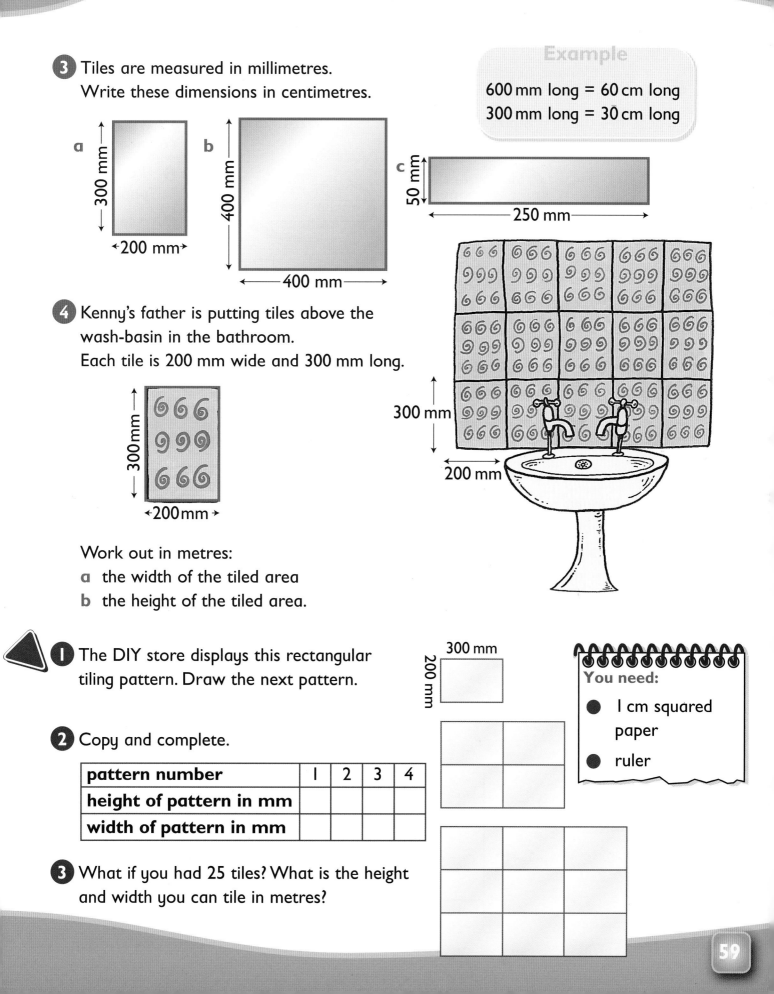

a   300 mm   ←200 mm→

b   400 mm   ←— 400 mm —→

c   50 mm   ←— 250 mm —→

4 Kenny's father is putting tiles above the
wash-basin in the bathroom.
Each tile is 200 mm wide and 300 mm long.

300 mm   ←200 mm→

300 mm

200 mm

Work out in metres:
a the width of the tiled area
b the height of the tiled area.

1 The DIY store displays this rectangular
tiling pattern. Draw the next pattern.

300 mm
200 mm

You need:
● I cm squared
   paper
● ruler

2 Copy and complete.

pattern number	I	2	3	4
height of pattern in mm				
width of pattern in mm				

3 What if you had 25 tiles? What is the height
and width you can tile in metres?

59

Pizzas

These are the first 8 pizzas bought from Pepe's Pizza Parlour on one day.

You need:
- I cm squared paper
- ruler

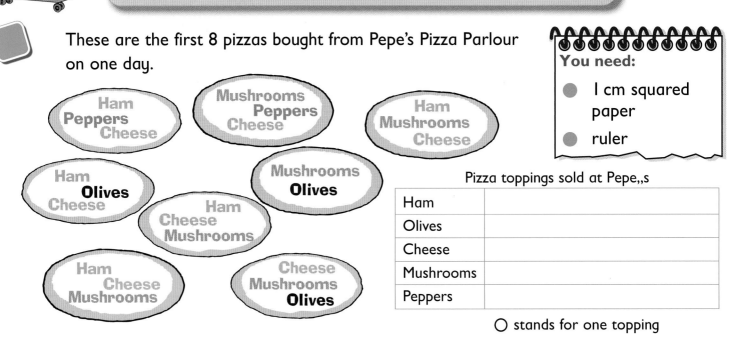

Pizza toppings sold at Pepe,,s

Ham	
Olives	
Cheese	
Mushrooms	
Peppers	

○ stands for one topping

1 Copy and complete the pictogram above. Draw a circle for each topping.

2 Use the information presented in the pictogram to answer these questions:
   a How many pizzas have ham topping?
   b How many more mushroom toppings than peppers toppings are there?
   c What is the most popular topping?
   d What is the least popular topping?

These are the next 8 pizzas bought from Pepe's Pizza Parlour.

You need:
- I cm squared paper
- ruler

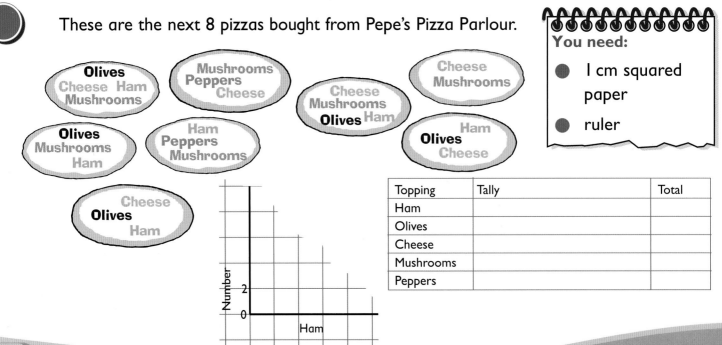

Topping	Tally	Total
Ham		
Olives		
Cheese		
Mushrooms		
Peppers		

1 Copy and complete the tally chart for all 16 pizzas. Draw a circle for every two toppings.

2 Copy and complete the bar chart.

3 Use the information presented in the bar chart to answer these questions:

    a Which is more popular: mushrooms or ham?

    b How many of all the pizzas sold had olives toppings?

    c Is the most popular topping still the same as question **2** c in the ◻ activity?

    d Is the least popular topping still the same as question **2** d in the ◻ activity?

The table below shows the pizza toppings sold by Pepe for a whole day.

Pizza topping	Number
Ham	36
Olives	26
Cheese	74
Mushrooms	53
Peppers	17

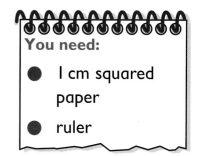

You need:
- 1 cm squared paper
- ruler

1 Present the information in the table above in a bar chart.

2 Use the information presented in the bar chart to answer these questions:

    a How many more mushroom toppings are there compared to olives toppings?
    b How many cheese and peppers toppings did Pepe sell?
    c How many toppings did Pepe sell altogether?
    d How many toppings are not cheese?

3 Write a sentence comparing your bar chart with the bar chart in the ● activity.

Ticket inspection

Find the mode for a set of data

1 What is the mode for each set of data?

a A, B, C, C, D

b 2, 5, 6, 6, 6, 7, 8

c 3, 3, 3, 4, 6, 7

d 10, 20, 20, 30, 30, 30

e 6, 2, 1, 5, 2, 2

f 1, 6, 1, 6, 1

g 100, 200, 400, 200, 100, 200

h L, M, N, L, N, L

2 What are the two modes for each set of data?

a P, P, O, R, R, S

b 2, 5, 5, 7, 7, 9

c 8, 8, 1, 4, 4, 3

d 10, 2, 1, 10, 2, 3

e 20, 40, 30, 30, 40, 10

f C, E, C, D, D, F

1 What is the mode of the ticket colours for each of the following sets?

What is the mode of the ticket prices for each of the following sets?

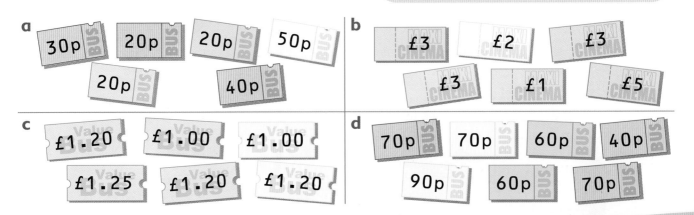

Example

£2   £4   £5   £1   £4

mode of colours is blue
mode of prices is £4

a

30p 20p 20p 50p
   20p   40p

b

£3   £2   £3
   £3   £1   £5

c

£1.20 £1.00 £1.00
   £1.25 £1.20 £1.20

d

70p 70p 60p 40p
   90p 60p 70p

2 Find the mode of the ticket colours. There may be two modes.

Find the mode of the ticket prices. There may be two modes or no mode.

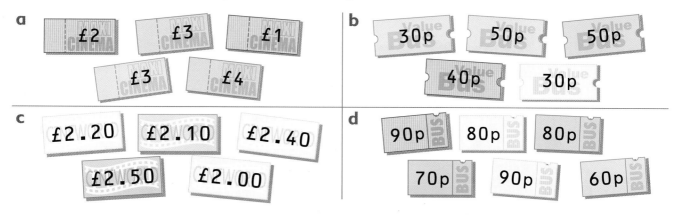

a
£2 £3 £1
£3 £4

b
30p 50p 50p
40p 30p

c
£2.20 £2.10 £2.40
£2.50 £2.00

d
90p 80p 80p
70p 90p 60p

3 Find the mode for each set of ticket prices.

a

Cinema ticket	Number of tickets
£5	3
£6	9
£7	24
£8	30
£9	15
£10	7

b

Taxi fare	Number of tickets
£1.50	0
£2.00	6
£2.50	11
£3.00	9
£3.50	11
£4.00	16

c

Aeroplane ticket	Number of tickets
£90	34
£130	42
£200	16
£240	5
£275	3
£340	0

1 Work with a partner.

Each person rolls the dice 10 times.
Multiply the numbers by 10
to get bus fares.

You need:
● 0-9 dice

Example

4 x 10 = 40p bus fare

2 What is the mode for your own set
of fares?

3 Compare your sets of fares.

Practical mode

Bumper cars

Your group needs:
- different coloured counter for each player
- 1-6 dice
- RCM 3: Bumper cars

A game for about 4 players.

1 Each player chooses a counter. This is your bumper car.

2 Each player places their car on a space marked S for 'Start'.

3 Take turns to roll the dice and move your car the same number of spaces in any direction. Try to move into a space next to another car. You might be able to crash into two cars like this.

4 Make a tally mark to record the colour of each car you crash into.

5 After five turns each, count the tally marks and write down the totals.

6 Which colour is the mode? What does the mode tell you?

Work with a partner.

Investigate how many cubes you can balance on the palm of your hand.

You each need:
- number of interlocking cubes

1 Take turns to balance as many cubes as you can on the palm of your hand.

2 Count each cube as it is placed.

3 Stop when a cube falls off.

4 Write down the total number of cubes you can balance each time.

5 Each person does this five times.

6 Record the number in the table.

	Number of cubes	
	Leah	Sarah
1		
2		
3		
4		
5		

7 What is the mode? What does this tell you?

Some children recorded how long they could balance a ruler on one finger before it fell.
They recorded the times, before and after some practice, in these two tables.

Before practice	
Time (seconds)	Number
1	2
2	2
3	6
4	3
5	0
6	1

After practice	
Time (seconds)	Number
3	1
4	2
5	4
6	5
7	1
8	0
9	1

1 Find the mode for each table.

2 Write two sentences comparing the results.

3 Do you think the children improved with practice? Explain your answer.

Stamp charts

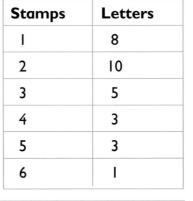

The table shows the number of stamps on letters arriving from overseas.

Stamps	Letters
1	8
2	10
3	5
4	3
5	3
6	1

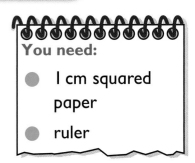

You need:
- 1 cm squared paper
- ruler

1 Copy and complete the bar line chart.

Stamps on letters from overseas

(y-axis: Letters, 0 to 10; x-axis: Stamps, 1 to 6)

2 What does the tallest bar line mean?

Karin recorded the numbers of letters posted through her letterbox each day.

1 What is the mode?

2 On how many days did Karin receive more than 5 letters?

Letters	Days
0	5
1	14
2	16
3	22
4	15
5	11
6	7
7	3

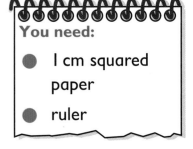

You need:
- 1 cm squared paper
- ruler

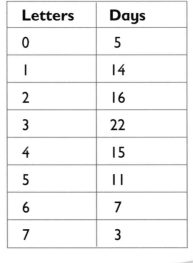

3 Copy and complete the bar line chart.

4 Choose your own scale for the vertical axis. Make sure your chart fits the paper.

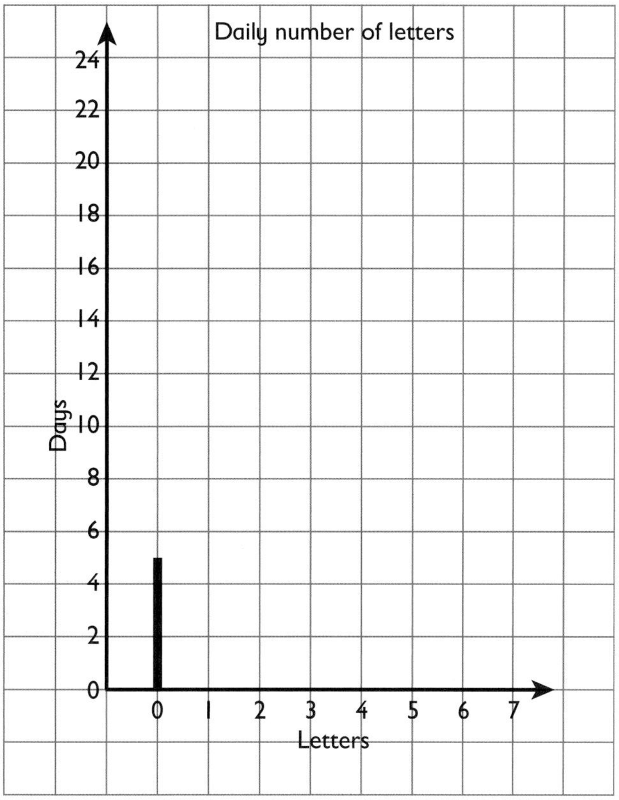

Daily number of letters

(bar line chart with vertical axis labelled "Days" marked 0, 2, 4, 6, 8, 10, 12, 14, 16, 18, 20, 22, 24 and horizontal axis labelled "Letters" marked 0, 1, 2, 3, 4, 5, 6, 7; one line drawn at 0 reaching 5)

The table shows the way some letters were sent.

1 Draw a bar chart for the data.

2 Draw a bar line chart for the data.

3 Draw a pictogram for the data.

4 Which diagram was quickest to draw?

5 Which diagram is easiest to read?

6 Which chart do you think represents the data best? Why?

postage	Letters
1st class	21
2nd class	26
Recorded	11
Special	5
Airmail	8

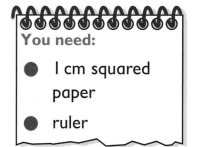

You need:

● 1 cm squared paper

● ruler

Bird bar line charts

Use graphs to explain answers to questions

You need:

- 1 cm squared paper
- ruler

1 The bar line chart shows the birds Dianne spotted. Copy and complete the table.

Bird	Number
thrush	
blackbird	
sparrow	
starling	
robin	

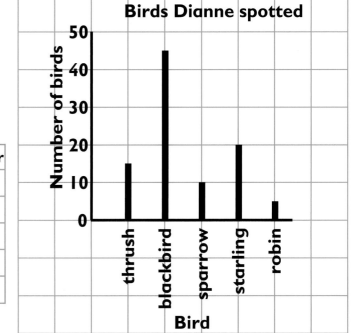

2 The table shows the birds Atul spotted. Copy and complete the bar line chart onto 1 cm squared paper.

Bird	Number
thrush	40
blackbird	75
sparrow	20
starling	35
robin	15

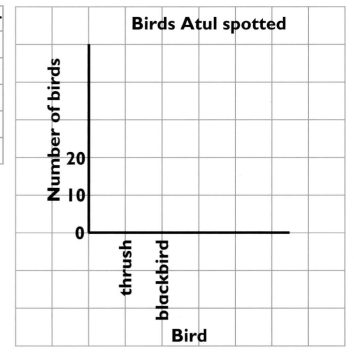

3 a How many starlings did Dianne spot?

b How many robins did Atul spot?

c Which bird did Dianne spot most?

d Which bird did Atul spot 35 times?

e Atul spotted more thrushes than Dianne. How many more?

f How many birds did Dianne spot altogether?

1. The bar line chart shows the worms collected by blackbirds.
Copy and complete the table.

You need:
- graph paper
- ruler

Worms	Number of times collected
1	
2	
3	
4	
5	
6	

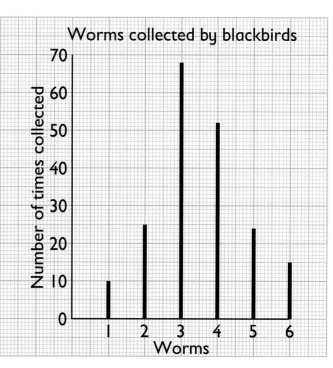

2. The table shows the worms collected by sparrows. Copy and complete the bar line chart onto graph paper.

Worms	Number of times collected
1	15
2	70
3	49
4	22
5	5

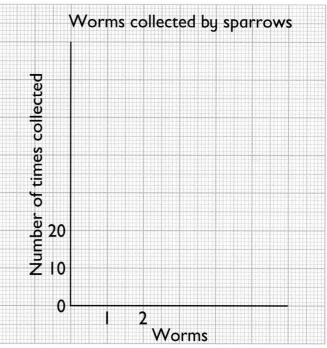

3. a How many blackbirds collected 3 worms?
   b Did more or fewer sparrows collect 3 worms?
   c What is the most common number of worms collected by blackbirds?
   d What is the mode for sparrows?
   e How many blackbirds collected fewer than 4 worms?
   f How many times did sparrows visit the garden altogether?

Combine Dianne and Atul's results from the ▢ activity. Draw a bar line chart. Number the vertical axis in steps of 20.

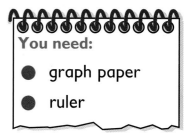

You need:
- graph paper
- ruler

Buttons

Construct pictograms, bar and bar line charts to represent the frequencies of events

The diagram shows 75 shirt buttons found in a sewing box.

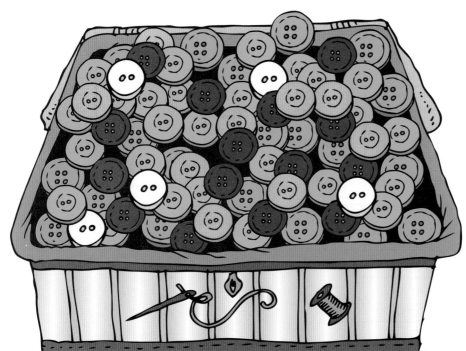

You need:

- 1 cm squared paper
- ruler

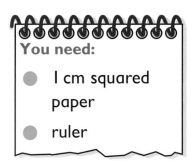

1. Count the buttons of each colour. Write the totals in a table.

2. Copy and complete the pictogram.

Colours of buttons

Red	
Green	
Blue	
Yellow	
White	

Number of buttons

△ stands for 5 buttons

3. What is the mode of the button colours?

You are going to investigate the sizes of a collection of buttons. Work in groups of four.

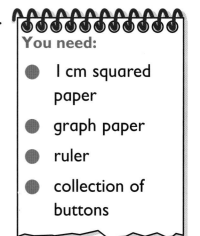

You need:
- 1 cm squared paper
- graph paper
- ruler
- collection of buttons

1. Each person chooses a quarter of the buttons and measures their widths, to the nearest mm. Record your measurements using a tally chart for the group.

2. Draw a bar chart using squared paper.

3. Draw a bar line chart using graph paper.

4. Which chart do you prefer? Explain why.

5. What is the mode of the button widths?

6. How many buttons have a width greater than the mode?

7. Measure the width of one of your buttons.
   Compare it to the mode.

The table shows the widths of some coat buttons.
Draw a bar line chart for the data.

Width (mm)	Number
23	18
24	34
25	48
26	78
27	144
28	96

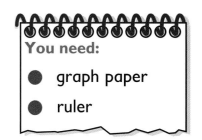

You need:
- graph paper
- ruler

Investigations

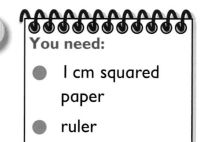

You need:
- 1 cm squared paper
- ruler

1 Write down the first name of everyone in the class. Make sure you spell the names correctly.

2 Make a tally mark for each vowel (a, e, i, o, u).

Vowel	Tally	Total
a		
e		
i		
o		
u		

3 Count the tally marks and write down the totals.

4 Copy and complete the bar line chart.

5 What is the mode?

6 Which is the least common vowel?

Vowels in first names

Number of names (y-axis: 0, 2, 4, 6, 8, 10, 12, 14)

Vowel (x-axis: a, e, i, o, u)

Work in a group.

1 Carry out an investigation to answer one of the following questions.

What is the most common number of letters in our first names?
Are girls' names longer than boys' names?
Do girls' names contain more syllables than boys' names?

How many vowels are there in most first names?

You need:
- 1 cm squared paper
- graph paper
- ruler

2 Decide what data you need to collect. Make sure there is enough time to collect the data.

3 Decide how your group will collect the data.

4 Record the data collected by the group using a tally chart.

5 Draw charts to show your data.

6 Use your data to answer the question.

7 After completing the investigation, discuss with the group how it could be improved.

Work in a group.

1 Think up your own question for the group to investigate.

2 Discuss each idea and decide which one to carry out. Make sure there is enough time to collect the data.

3 Plan the investigation. Solve any practical problems. Decide who will do what.

4 Decide how to collect and record the data.

5 Draw charts to show your data.

6 Use your data to answer the question.

7 After completing the investigation, discuss with the group how it could be improved.

You need:
- 1 cm squared paper
- graph paper
- ruler

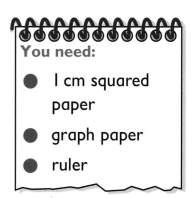

10, 100 and 1000 again

Multiply and divide by 10, 100 or 1000 and understand the effect

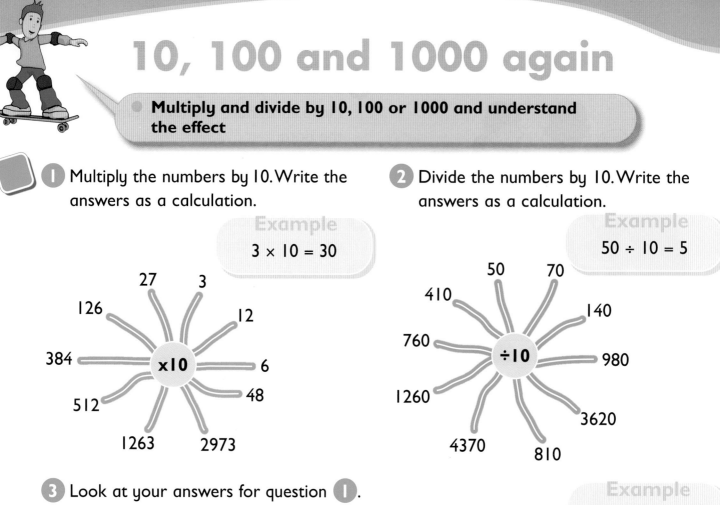

1 Multiply the numbers by 10. Write the answers as a calculation.

Example
3 × 10 = 30

27   3
126   12
384   ×10   6
512   48
1263   2973

2 Divide the numbers by 10. Write the answers as a calculation.

Example
50 ÷ 10 = 5

50   70
410   140
760   ÷10   980
1260   3620
4370   810

3 Look at your answers for question **1**.
Divide each of these answers by 100.

Example
30 ÷ 100 = 0·3

1 Copy and complete the tables.

a

Number	×10	×100
287	2870	28 700
165		
8911		
5126		
3864		

b

Number	×100	×1000
8	800	8000
28		
263		
594		
812		

c

Number	÷10	÷100
400	40	4
2700		
31 900		
4320		
5610		

d

Number	÷100	÷1000
5000	50	5
6200		
21 700		
1400		
3800		

74

2 Each of the following calculations have either been multiplied or divided by 10, 100 or 1000. Copy and complete.

a 99 ☐ = 9900

b 500 ☐ = 50

c 57 200 ☐ = 57·2

d 2729 ☐ = 27 290

e 1680 ☐ = 168 000

f 41 300 ☐ = 4130

g 729 400 ☐ = 7294

h 260 ☐ = 26 000

i 560 ☐ = 560 000

j 270 ☐ = 2·7

k 41 320 ☐ = 4132

l 4500 ☐ = 45 000

m 217 ☐ = 217 000

n 12 960 ☐ = 1296

o 6831 ☐ = 683 100

p 19 500 ☐ = 19·5

q 25 800 ☐ = 258

r 9243 ☐ = 92 430

s 120 ☐ = 1200

t 812 300 ☐ = 812·3

Example

630 ☐ = 6·3

630 ÷ 100 = 6·3

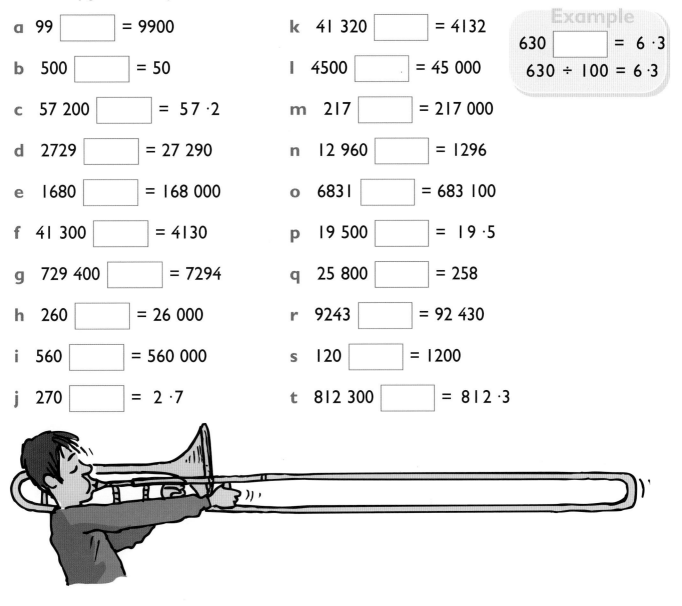

Answer these questions using your knowledge of multiplying and dividing by 10, 100 and 1000. Show all your working.

a How many times larger is 37 000 than 37?

b How many £10 notes in £360?

c A bar of chocolate costs 39p. How much would ten bars cost?

d How many times larger is 4900 than 4·9 ?

e 100 packets of biscuits cost £48. How much does one packet cost?

Solving word problems

Solve word problems involving one or more steps

Write the calculation needed to answer each of these problems.

a The Roberts family are going on holiday in six weeks' time. How many days is that?

> **Example**
>
> 6 × 7 = 42

b The Kruger family are going on holiday for four weeks. How many days will they be away for?

c Sarah and John have saved a total of £28 between them. How much have they saved each?

e Simone gets £7 for washing the family car. She has saved a total of £56. How many times has she washed the car?

d Joanne gets £5 pocket money per week. She has saved up for nine weeks. How much money does she have?

f There are four people in the Roberts family. Mum buys one bottle of sunscreen per person. Each bottle costs £6. What is the total cost?

Read the word problems. Choose an appropriate method of calculating your answers.

Remember

You will need to use the answers from some questions to help you calculate other answers!

The Roberts family

Sarah   John

a A taxi to the airport will cost the Kruger family £40. The airport train costs £9·50 for adults and £6 for children. Which is the cheaper option and by how much?

b The Roberts family drive to the airport. Parking costs £5·80 per day for the first seven days and £4·60 per day after that. How much does car parking cost for their ten-day holiday?

76

The Kruger family

Joanne James
Simone Bobby

c The Kruger family need to purchase travel insurance. Family cover costs £235. Separate cover costs £58 for adults and £34 for children. Which cover will cost the family the least and by how much?

d Is it cheaper for the Roberts family to take their car to the airport or to catch the train to the airport and back? What is the difference in price?

e Both families travel on the same plane. The cost of the flight for the adults is £368 per person and £177 per child. What is the total cost for both families together?

f The Kruger family book their plane seats in advance. They are charged an extra £26 per person. How much extra do they pay altogether?

Use the information in the ● activity to plan a 7 day holiday for the Patel family (2 adults, 3 children). They have a budget of £2000. Find the cheapest options to enable them to stick to their budget.

a Draw up a price list.

Taxi:........

Airport train........

Parking:.........

Insurance:........

Flights:.........

b Find the cheapest transport to and from the airport.

c Find the cost of flights.

d Prepare a final invoice listing the costs of each item and the final price.

INVOICE

Transport:.........

Flights:.........

Insurance:........

Total:........

Lengths and distances

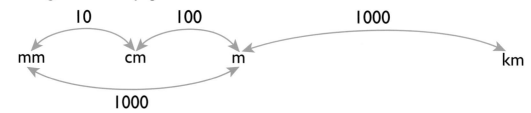

● Choose and use appropriate number operations to solve problems involving length

Use this diagram to help you.

```
        10            100              1000
   ⌒⌒⌒⌒⌒⌒    ⌒⌒⌒⌒⌒⌒         ⌒⌒⌒⌒⌒⌒⌒⌒⌒
  mm          cm          m                    km
   ⌣⌣⌣⌣⌣⌣⌣⌣⌣⌣⌣⌣
        1000
```

1 Write these sentences choosing the best measurement to make them correct.

  a The eraser is about ☐ long.   5 mm   55 mm   555 mm

  b The fence is about ☐ tall.   10 cm   100 cm   1000 cm

  c The classroom is about ☐ high. 3 m   6 m   12 m

  d My uncle is about ☐ tall.   1·93 m   19·3 m   193 m

2 Three children took part in a sunflower growing competition.
Here are their results.

Steven	2000 mm
Hannah	204 cm
Sienna	2·02 m

You need:
● calculator

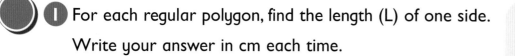

  a Who grew the winning sunflower?

  b By how many millimetres did it win?

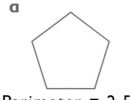**1** For each regular polygon, find the length (L) of one side.

Write your answer in cm each time.

Example

L = 1·6 m ÷ 4
= 160 cm ÷ 4
= 40 cm
One side = 40 m

  a   **b**   **c**   **d**

Perimeter = 2·5 m   Perimeter = 0·9 m   Perimeter = 4·8 m   Perimeter = 5·6 m

2 Fingernails grow about 1 mm each week. If you never cut your nails, how long would they be:

a 1 year from now?

b 10 years from now?

3 **a** Pat's stride measures about 50 cm. She lives about 500 m from school. Approximately how many strides does she take walking from home to school?

b A Roman pace is a person's stride doubled. How many Roman paces does Pat take for the same distance?

4 Marco is driving in Italy. He sees this road sign. About how many miles is it To Naples? To Pompeii? To Sorrento?

To find the answer, enter this key sequence into your calculator:

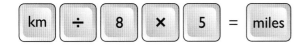

Naples 48 km
Pompeii 40 km
Sorrento 24 km

Joanne is making Christmas decorations. She needs a piece of ribbon 39 cm long but she cannot find her measuring tape. Earlier she cut 3 lengths of ribbon measuring 31 cm, 33 cm and 37 cm. Explain how she uses the 3 pieces to measure the length of ribbon she needs.

Between lengths

Draw and measure in millimetres

1 Estimate and measure these objects to the nearest millimetre.

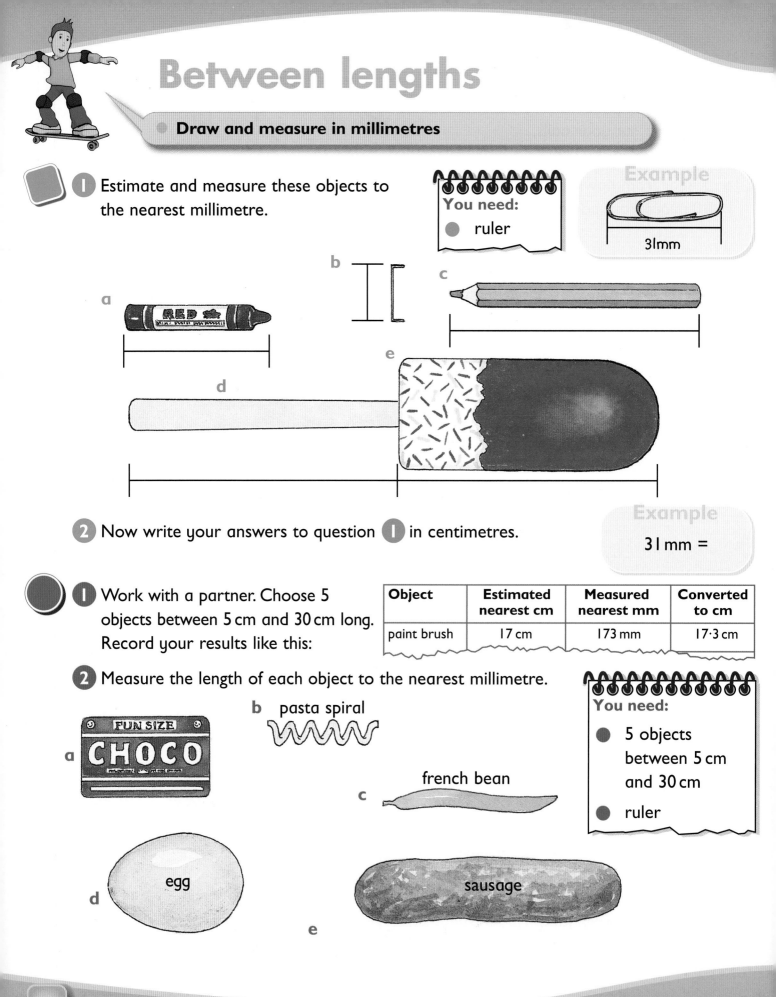

You need:
● ruler

Example

31mm

a RED

b

c

d

e

2 Now write your answers to question ① in centimetres.

Example

31 mm =

① Work with a partner. Choose 5 objects between 5 cm and 30 cm long. Record your results like this:

Object	Estimated nearest cm	Measured nearest mm	Converted to cm
paint brush	17 cm	173 mm	17·3 cm

2 Measure the length of each object to the nearest millimetre.

a FUN SIZE CHOCO

b pasta spiral

c french bean

d egg

e sausage

You need:
● 5 objects between 5 cm and 30 cm
● ruler

80

3 For each object in question **2**, work out the total length, in centimetres, of a straight line of 10 identical objects.

4 Work out the length of each key by calculating the distance between the two arrows. Using decimal notation, record your answers in centimetres.

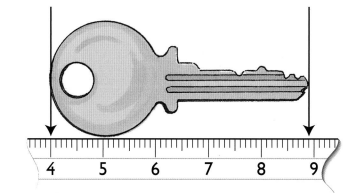

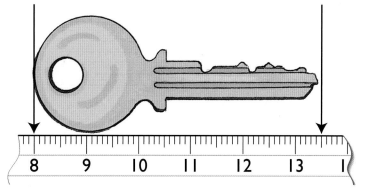

Alison needs four white buttons of the same size for a baby jacket she has knitted. This is her collection of buttons.

You need:
● ruler

Which size of button does she choose?

Rectangle round up

Mrs Trayner made this display of photographs of her grandchildren. Calculate the perimeter of each photograph in cm. Show how you worked it out.

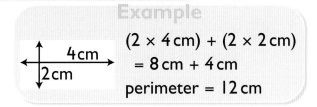

Example

$(2 × 4\,cm) + (2 × 2\,cm)$
$= 8\,cm + 4\,cm$
perimeter = 12 cm

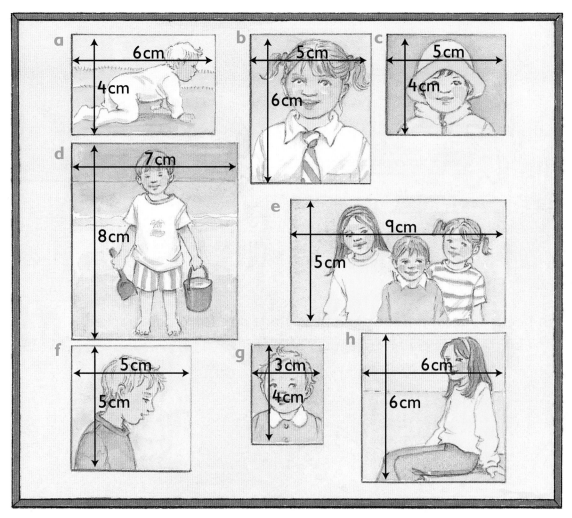

a 6 cm 4 cm

b 5 cm 6 cm

c 5 cm 4 cm

d 7 cm 8 cm

e 9 cm 5 cm

f 5 cm 5 cm

g 3 cm 4 cm

h 6 cm 6 cm

1 Copy and complete these rectangles on 1 cm squared paper. The perimeters are given for each rectangle.

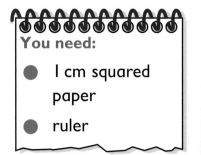

You need:
● 1 cm squared paper
● ruler

a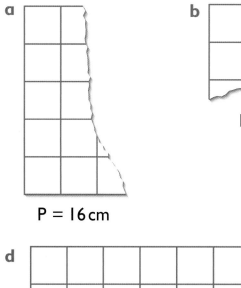

P = 16 cm

b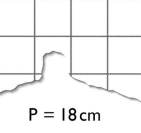

P = 18 cm

c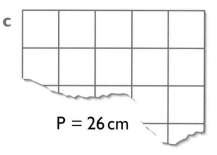

P = 26 cm

d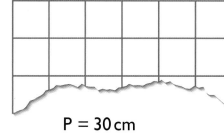

P = 30 cm

e

P = 28 cm

f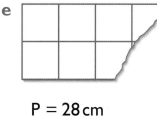

P = 20 cm

2 Find three different ways to complete this rectangle.

P = 24 cm

3 Construct 5 rectangles each with a perimeter of 22 cm.

4 The perimeter of a rectangle is 60 cm. The shorter side is 9 cm. What is the length of the longer side?

Work with a partner.

You have 9 squares, each with sides of 2 cm. What is the largest perimeter you can make? What is the smallest?

Regular perimeters

Understand, measure and calculate perimeters of rectangles and regular polygons

① Use your ruler and measure the perimeter of these shapes. Show all your working.

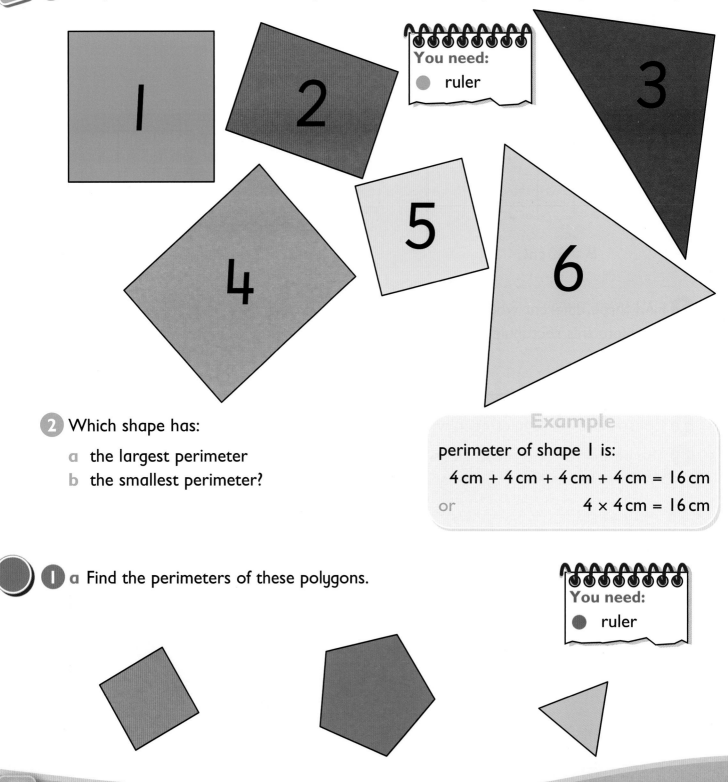

You need:
● ruler

1

2

3

4

5

6

② Which shape has:

a the largest perimeter
b the smallest perimeter?

perimeter of shape 1 is:

$4\,cm + 4\,cm + 4\,cm + 4\,cm = 16\,cm$

or $4 \times 4\,cm = 16\,cm$

① a Find the perimeters of these polygons.

You need:
● ruler

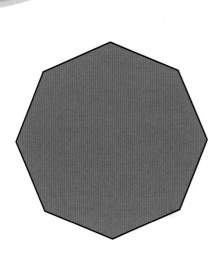
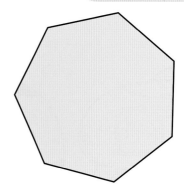

b Copy and complete the table.

number of sides of polygon	3	4	5	6	7	8
perimeter in cm						

2 Explain why the perimeter of the hexagon is double that of the triangle.

3 Write what you notice about the perimeters of the square and the octagon.

4 If you continue the pattern, what will the perimeter be for:
a 10-sided regular shape?
a 15-sided regular shape?

These regular hexagons have sides of 1 cm.
They make this pattern of shapes.

HINT

Draw the first 6 patterns on 1 cm hexagonal grid paper. Then make a table.

You need:
● 1 cm hexagonal grid paper
● ruler

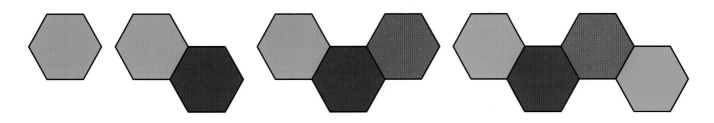

What is the perimeter of the pattern of 10 regular hexagons?

24-hour clocks

❶ Write 24-hour times for:

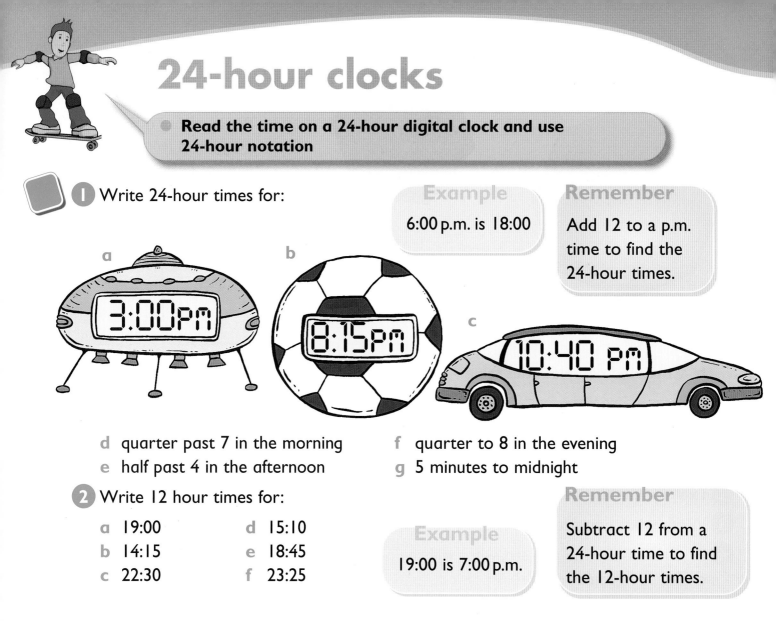

Example

6:00 p.m. is 18:00

Remember

Add 12 to a p.m. time to find the 24-hour times.

a **3:00pm**

b **8:15pm**

c **10:40 pm**

d quarter past 7 in the morning

e half past 4 in the afternoon

f quarter to 8 in the evening

g 5 minutes to midnight

❷ Write 12 hour times for:

a 19:00   d 15:10

b 14:15   e 18:45

c 22:30   f 23:25

Example

19:00 is 7:00 p.m.

Remember

Subtract 12 from a 24-hour time to find the 12-hour times.

 ❶ Copy and complete this chart.

Time	12-hour clock	24-hour clock
half past 7 in the morning	7:30 a.m.	07:30
	10:05 a.m.	
		13:25
quarter to 9 in the evening		
	9:25 p.m.	
		22:40
10 minutes past midnight		
	2:47 a.m.	
		20:35

2 Look at the aircraft landing times on the TV monitor.

a Write the timetabled time for each plane as 12-hour times. Add a.m. or p.m.

b Look at the 'Remarks' column. Work out the 12-hour landing times for the flights from Toronto, Paris and Brussels.

Timetabled time		Remarks
08:20	Heathrow	Landed
09:45	Toronto	Delayed 10:20
10:00	Chicago	Landed
12:45	Manchester	Landed
13:10	Paris (CDG)	Expected 12:55
14:45	Brussels	Expected 15:10

Ships at sea must have officers on duty at all times. The 24-hour day is divided into watches and the officers take turns to be on duty.

Make up a duty roster for the captain (C), first officer (O) and 3 junior officers (J, K and L). You must observe the following rules:

Example		
Time	**Watch**	**Officers**
00:00	Middle	O, J
04:00	Morning	

- 2 people on duty at all times.
- No watch should be longer than 6 hours.
- No officer can do more than 12 hours duty in a 24-hour period.
- The captain and first officer are on different watches.

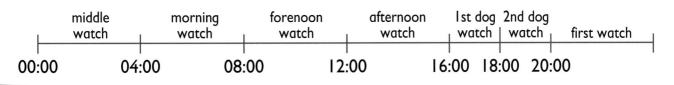

middle watch	morning watch	forenoon watch	afternoon watch	1st dog watch	2nd dog watch	first watch
00:00	04:00	08:00	12:00	16:00	18:00	20:00

Calculating times

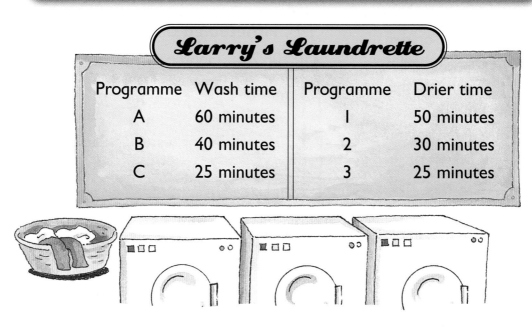

Larry's Laundrette

Programme	Wash time	Programme	Drier time
A	60 minutes	1	50 minutes
B	40 minutes	2	30 minutes
C	25 minutes	3	25 minutes

1 For each of these customers:

- work out how long it took to wash and dry clothes
- write the time in 24-hour notation when their laundry was finished.

a Mrs Gray arrived at 14:00 and used wash programme A and drier programme 2.

b Mr White arrived at 15:15 and used wash programme C and drier programme 3.

c Miss Green arrived at 16:50 and used wash programme B and drier programme 3.

2 Mrs Brown finished her laundry at 20:30. She used programme C for washing and programme 1 for drying. At what time on the 12-hour clock did she come into the laundrette?

 Peter is planning his holiday for next year. He makes a list of things he would like to do. He jots down these timings from the holiday brochure.

Activity	Start time	Finish time
Pioneer train trip	11:00	15:30
White water rafting	08:30	13:00
Guided forest hike	10:00	12:15
Hot air ballooning	14:45	17:30
Mountain biking trail	09:00	11:45
Hot springs swimming	16:30	18:30
Lakeside canoeing	13:45	16:15

Use this time line to help you.

08:00 10:00 12:00 14:00 16:00 18:00 19:00

1 Which activity takes the shortest time?

2 Which activity starts at quarter to 2 in the afternoon?

3 Which activity finishes at half past 5 in the evening?

4 List two activities Peter can do on the same day. How long will each activity last?

5 This activity will take four and a half hours to complete. What is it?

6 Lift-off for the hot air balloon is delayed by 35 minutes. What are the new starting and finishing times?

7 After 50 minutes paddling his canoe, Peter stops to take some photographs. What time will his analogue watch show? His camera records the time in the 12-hour clock. What time will be printed on his photographs?

You are cooking a meal for the family. Work out the starting times for the turkey, the potatoes and the vegetables so that the meal is ready to eat at 18:00.

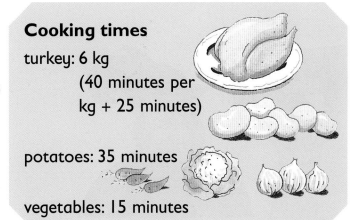

Cooking times

turkey: 6 kg
(40 minutes per kg + 25 minutes)

potatoes: 35 minutes

vegetables: 15 minutes

Puzzle time

1 a Copy this year's calendar for the month of February.

 b Circle the days when the Fontana Museum is open.

2 On which days throughout the year is the museum open?

3 On which day is it closed every month of the year?

4 For how many months is the museum open on Thursdays?

5 In which months is it closed on a Wednesday?

You need:

● this year's calendar

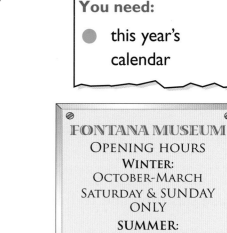

FONTANA MUSEUM
OPENING HOURS
WINTER:
OCTOBER–MARCH
SATURDAY & SUNDAY
ONLY
SUMMER:
APRIL–SEPTEMBER
DAILY, EXCEPT TUESDAYS

1 Write the leap years between 1980 and 2020.

2 Write the date for these days in a year which is not a leap year.

 a 50th day **b** 100th day **c** 150th day **d** 200th day

3 Carole's birthday is on 24 June. On which day of the week is it?

HINT

2000 was a leap year.

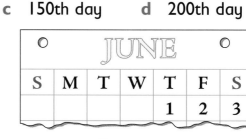

S	M	T	W	T	F	S
				1	2	3

JUNE

4 Henry VIII's wife Anne was Queen for 1000 days. For how many years and days was she Queen?

5 You see this advert and buy a light bulb. If the company's claim is true, for how many weeks, days and hours should the light bulbs last?

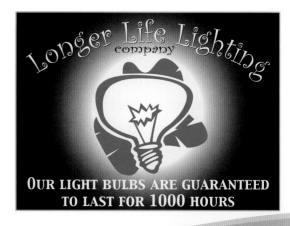

Longer Life Lighting
company

OUR LIGHT BULBS ARE GUARANTEED
TO LAST FOR 1000 HOURS

90

6 Jim drew a rectangle round 9 dates in September to make 3 rows of 3 dates. First he added 8 to the smallest number in the rectangle, and multiplied the answer by 9. Then he totalled all 9 numbers. He did this several times for other rectangles of 9 numbers. What did he discover? Investigate.

1 Use the information to work out the ages of these children.

Jack: I am 2 years younger than Terry.

Jo: I am a year older than Jack.

Katie: I am 3 years younger than Terry. I will be 10 next year.

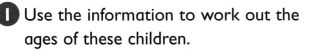

2 Rosie the dog and Bruce the puppy are mother and son. Bruce is now the same age that Rosie was 4 years ago. 4 years ago, Bruce was half his mother's age. Rosie is now 12 years old. What age is her son?

3 Ashrif was at a friend's birthday party on 20 March 2004.
'You're lucky,' he said to his friend, 'I'm also 12 years old but I've only had 3 proper birthdays.'
What is Ashrif's date of birth?

Plotting the points

These are the positions of some yachts during a race.

1. Write the co-ordinates of yachts A, B, C and D.

2. Write the co-ordinates for the following yachts.

   a The 2 yachts with x co-ordinate 2.

   b The 2 yachts with y co-ordinate 1.

   c The yacht with x co-ordinate zero.

   d The yacht with y co-ordinate zero.

   e The yacht with the same
   x and y co-ordinates.

Example

yacht A (2, 5)

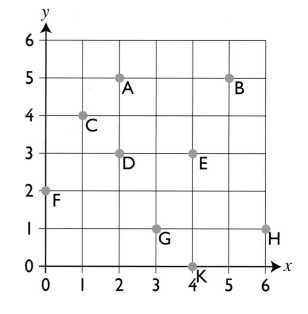

1. a Copy these points
   on to a 6 x 6
   co-ordinate grid.
   Write down the
   co-ordinates of each
   point.

   b Plot these points on
   the same grid.
   (3, 0), (3, 1), (3, 2), (3, 3), (3, 4), (3, 5)
   Draw a straight line through the points.
   Name the axis to which the line is parallel.

   c On the same grid, mark the points (0, 0) and
   (6, 6). Join them with a straight line. Write the
   co-ordinates of the points where the diagonal
   line crosses the other two lines.

You need:

● RCM 7: 6 × 6
co-ordinate grids

● RCM 8: 9 × 9
co-ordinate grids

Example

C (2, 4)

Example

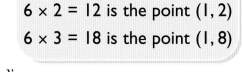

6 × 2 = 12 is the point (1, 2)

6 × 3 = 18 is the point (1, 8)

2 Some multiples of × 6 table are plotted on this grid.

a Copy these points on to a 9 × 9 co-ordinate grid.

b Continue as far as you can.

c Write the co-ordinates of the points where the pattern repeats.

3 a Copy and continue this table to 8 × 10.

Multiple	co-ordinates
8 × 1 = 8	(0, 8)
8 × 2 = 16	(1, 6)
8 × 3 = 24	(2, 4)

… and so on.

b Label the axes as in question **2**.

c Plot the points on another 9 × 9 co-ordinate grid.

d Write about patterns you notice.

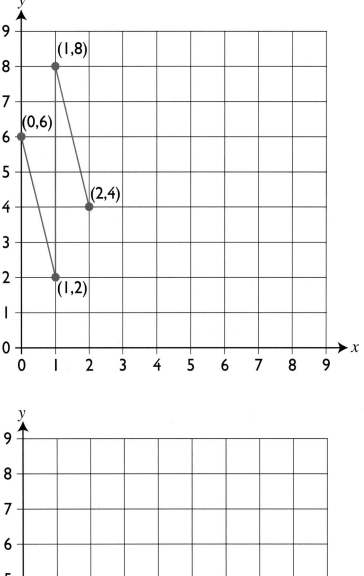

a Plot these points: (3, 0), (9, 6) and (3, 6).

b Join the points with straight lines.

c Write the co-ordinates of all the points the lines pass through.

You need:

● RCM 9: 9 × 9 co-ordinate grids

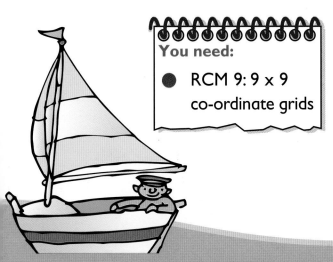

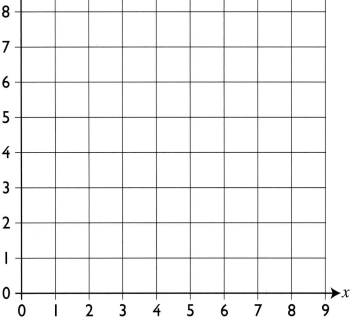

Are they equal?

1 How many sections would need to be shaded to make a half?

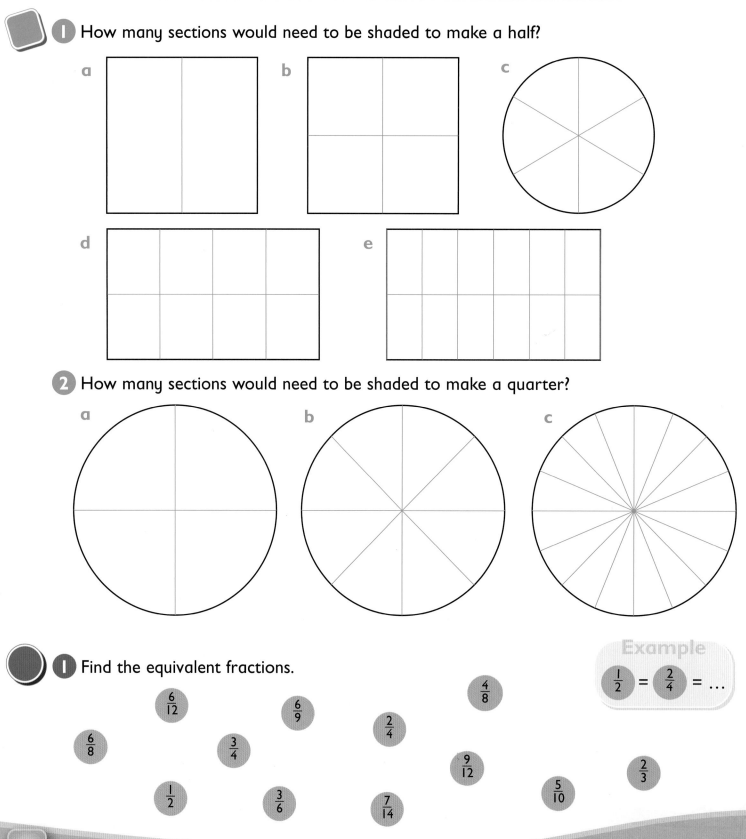

a

b

c

d

e

2 How many sections would need to be shaded to make a quarter?

a

b

c

1 Find the equivalent fractions.

$\frac{6}{12}$

$\frac{6}{9}$

$\frac{4}{8}$

$\frac{6}{8}$

$\frac{3}{4}$

$\frac{2}{4}$

$\frac{9}{12}$

$\frac{2}{3}$

$\frac{1}{2}$

$\frac{3}{6}$

$\frac{7}{14}$

$\frac{5}{10}$

Example

$\frac{1}{2}$ = $\frac{2}{4}$ = ...

94

2 Find the equivalent fractions for a third.

a b c

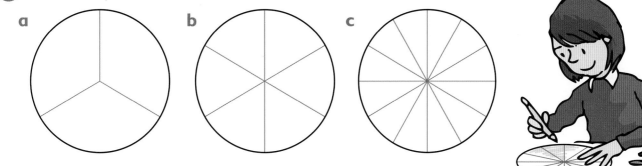

What patterns do you see in the equivalent fractions for a third?

3 Find the equivalent fractions for a fifth.

a b c

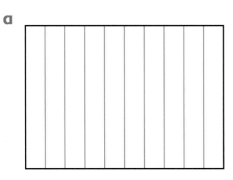

What patterns do you see in the equivalent fractions for a fifth?

4 Find the equivalent fractions for a tenth.

a b

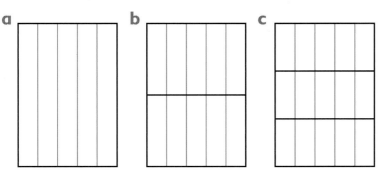

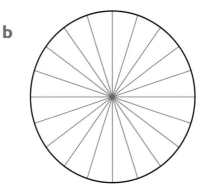

What patterns do you see in the equivalent fractions for a tenth?

 What fractions are equivalent to $\frac{1}{6}$?
What is the pattern?
Investigate other equivalent fractions.

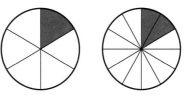

Example

$\frac{1}{6} = \frac{2}{12} = \ldots$

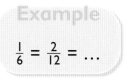

Fractions and decimals

1 Copy and complete the decimal number line from 0 to 1.

Remember

To draw both your number lines the same length.

0   0·1   1

2 Copy and complete the fraction number line from 0 to 1.

0      $\frac{1}{10}$ 1

3 Both of the number lines are in tenths. One is in decimals and one is in fractions. Use the number lines to find the equivalent decimal or fraction.

a $\frac{1}{10}$ b $\frac{4}{10}$ c $\frac{7}{10}$

d $\frac{9}{10}$ e $\frac{3}{10}$ f   0·6

g   0·8   h   0·5   i   0·2

4 What decimal is equivalent to $\frac{1}{2}$?

1 Copy the bar and number line for each question.
Colour the correct fraction of each bar and then put the equivalent decimal on the number line.

a $\frac{1}{2}$

0   1

b $\frac{1}{4}$

0   1

c $\frac{3}{4}$

0   1

d $\frac{6}{10}$

0   1

e $\frac{9}{10}$

0   1

f $\frac{2}{10}$

0   1

g $\frac{5}{10}$

0   1

2 What do you notice about the fraction you coloured in and where you have put the decimal equivalent on the number line?

1 Explain why there are equivalent decimals and fractions.

2 Design a number line that will help someone who is not sure about the equivalences between decimals and fractions.

3 Can you include fractions that are not on these two pages?

Fractions and division

Find fractions using division

1 Find half of these numbers and amounts.

a 14   b 26   c 48   d 100   e 140

f 500 g   g 60 minutes   h 208 km   i £700   j 90 cm

2 Find a quarter of these numbers and amounts.

a 40   b 16   c 24   d 100

e 84   f 400 m   g £36   h 60 g   i 800 km

3 Find a third of these numbers and amounts.

a 30   b 15   c 21

d 90   e 300   f 9 kg   g 600 km   h £27

1 Copy and complete the statements.

a To find halves you divide by ☐.

b To find thirds you divide by ☐.

c To find quarters you divide by ☐.

d To find tenths you divide by ☐.

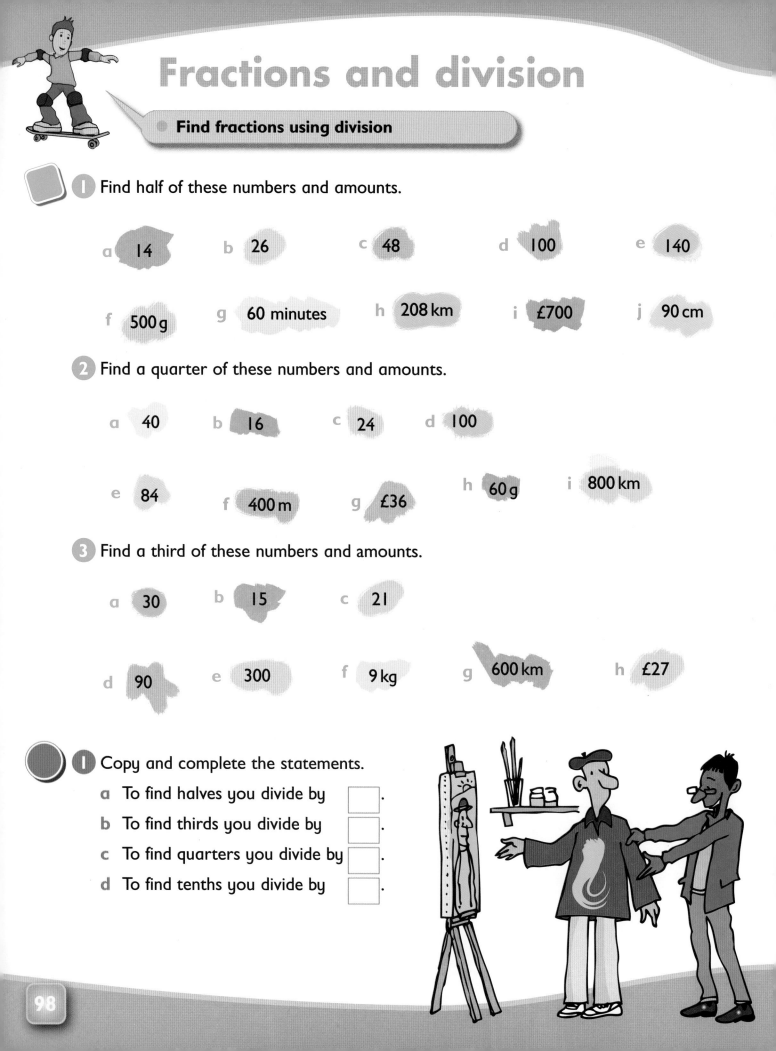

2 Work out the fractions of these numbers and amounts.
Write the division calculation for each one.

a $\frac{1}{2}$ of 16

b half of 60 kg

c $\frac{1}{2}$ of 84

d half of £5

e third of 90

f $\frac{1}{3}$ of 27 g

g quarter of £1

h $\frac{1}{4}$ of 240?

i Quarter of 280 ml

j third of 330 g

k $\frac{1}{3}$ of an hour

l $\frac{1}{4}$ of 1 kg

m $\frac{1}{10}$ of 700

n tenth of 420 ml

o $\frac{1}{10}$ of £1

p tenth of 11

3 Explain why fractions and division go together.

What is the number? Show your working.

a $\frac{1}{4}$ of the number is 3

b $\frac{1}{2}$ of the number is 46

c $\frac{1}{3}$ of the number is 99

d $\frac{1}{2}$ of the number is 34·5

e $\frac{1}{4}$ of the number is 153

f $\frac{1}{10}$ of the number is 37

g $\frac{1}{3}$ of the number is 0·4

h $\frac{1}{100}$ of the number is 3

i $\frac{1}{1000}$ of the number is 25

Percentages

Find percentages of numbers and quantities

What per cent of each grid has been shaded?
What per cent has not been shaded?

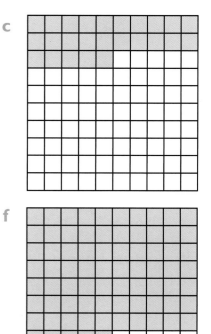

a

b

c

d

e

f

What per cent of each shape has been shaded?
What per cent has not been shaded?

Remember

100% is the whole amount.

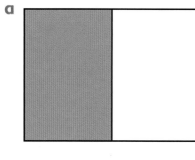

a

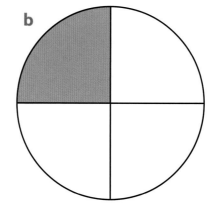

b

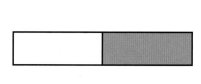

c

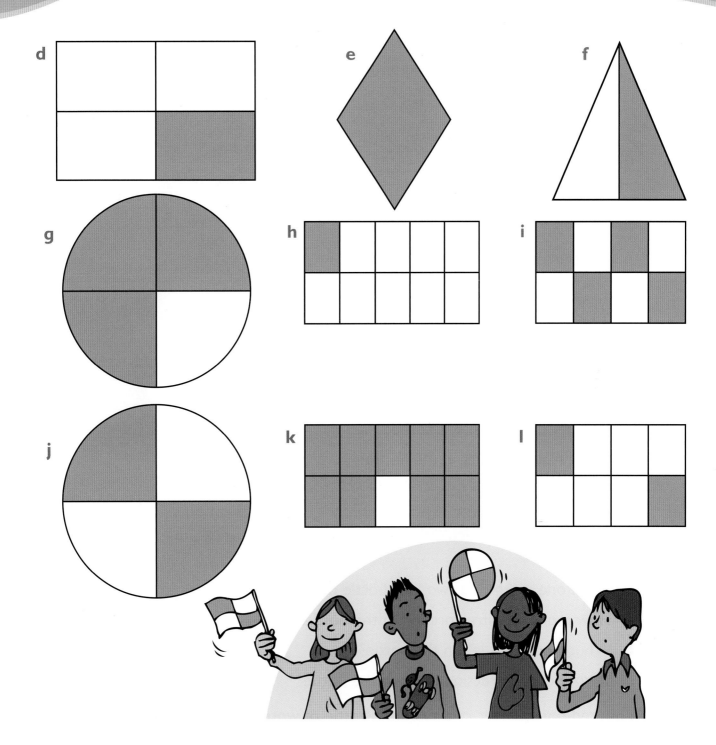

Write the percentages as fractions and decimals.

50%

25%

20%

75%

90%

30%

80%

40%

60%

70%

Liquid problems

> Solve one-step and two-step word problems involving fractions and decimals

Solve the word problems. Show all your workings.

1 I have 400 ml of juice.

a If I pour out $\frac{1}{2}$, how many ml is that?

b If I pour out $\frac{1}{4}$, how many ml is that?

c If I pour out $\frac{1}{10}$, how many ml is that?

2 I poured out one quarter of my 200 ml bottle of water.

a How many millilitres did I pour out?

b How much is left in the bottle?

c What fraction is left in the bottle?

Solve the word problems. Choose whether to work them out mentally or using a calculator. For both methods, show all your workings.

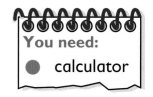

You need:
● calculator

1 I poured one tenth of a two litre bottle of water into a glass.

a How many millilitres are left in the bottle?

b What fraction is left in the bottle?

c What decimal fraction is left in the bottle?

2 I poured one quarter of a two litre bottle of water into a glass.

a How many millilitres are left in the bottle?

b What fraction is left in the bottle?

c If I had poured out three quarters of water how much would that be?

102

3 I poured out one seventh of a 672 ml bottle of water into a glass.

  a How many millilitres did I pour out?

  b What fraction is left in the bottle?

  c What if I had poured out $\frac{5}{7}$. How much would that be?

4 I had 225 ml of milk in my glass. This was $\frac{1}{5}$ of the whole carton.

  a How much was left in the carton?

  b What fraction was left in the carton?

  c What decimal fraction of the milk did I have in my glass?

I buy a carton of juice to share with my friends.

I drink 25% of it when I get home. Then I accidentally spill 0·2 of a litre.

I share out what is left between my three friends and myself and we all have 175 ml.

How much juice did I buy?

Multiplication and division facts

Know multiplication facts up to 10 x 10 and related division facts

Use multiplication facts to multiply pairs of multiples of 10 and 100

1 Copy and complete.

a   6 x 8 = ◯
b   5 x 7 = ◯
c   8 x 4 = ◯
d   6 x 6 = ◯
e   7 x 5 = ◯
f   4 x 9 = ◯
g   3 x 7 = ◯
h   9 x 2 = ◯

2 Copy and complete.

a   56 ÷ 8 = ◯
b   25 ÷ 5 = ◯
c   21 ÷ 3 = ◯
d   49 ÷ 7 = ◯
e   60 ÷ 6 = ◯
f   24 ÷ 3 = ◯
g   72 ÷ 9 = ◯
h   80 ÷ 10 = ◯

1 Copy and complete each set of calculations.

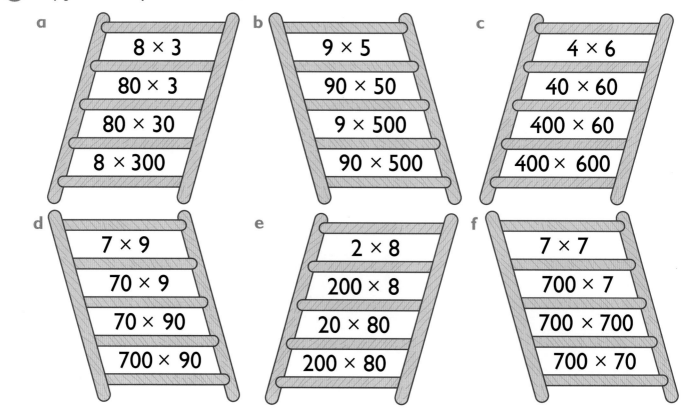

a
8 × 3
80 × 3
80 × 30
8 × 300

b
9 × 5
90 × 50
9 × 500
90 × 500

c
4 × 6
40 × 60
400 × 60
400 × 600

d
7 × 9
70 × 9
70 × 90
700 × 90

e
2 × 8
200 × 8
20 × 80
200 × 80

f
7 × 7
700 × 7
700 × 700
700 × 70

2 Use your knowledge of the times tables facts up to 10 x 10 to help you work out the answers to these calculations.

a 80 x 3 = ◯

b 6 x 90 = ◯

c 200 x ◯ = 1800

d 500 x ◯ = 250 000

e 6 x 300 = ◯

f 90 x ◯ = 54 000

g 400 x ◯ = 12 000

h 60 x 2 = ◯

i 90 x 100 = ◯

j 800 x ◯ = 24 000

k 4 x 40 = ◯

l 600 x ◯ = 1200

m 90 x 90 = ◯

n 300 x ◯ = 2700

o 200 x ◯ = 8000

p 400 x 40 = ◯

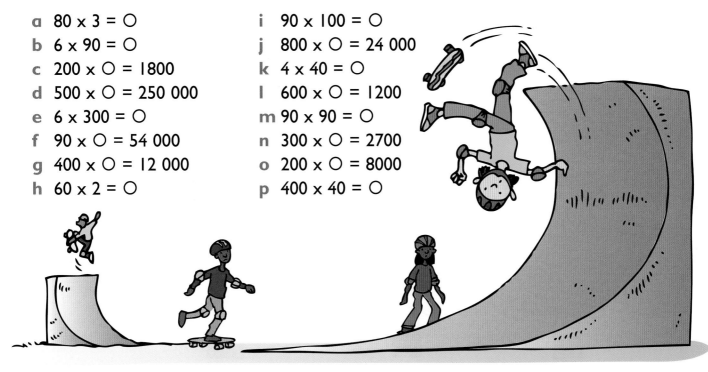

1 Copy and complete.

a 800 ÷ 20 = ◯

b 450 ÷ 5 = ◯

c 42 000 ÷ ◯ = 70

d 270 ÷ ◯ = 9

e 3200 ÷ ◯ = 80

f 480 000 ÷ 600 = ◯

g 36 000 ÷ ◯ = 90

h 1400 ÷ 20 = ◯

i 9000 ÷ ◯ = 300

j 400 000 ÷ ◯ = 500

2 For each of the numbers below, write as many different calculations as you can that involve multiplying pairs of multiples of 10 and 100.

2400 360 560 000 120 000 48 000

Factor trees

Find all the pairs of factors of any numbers up to 100

Search each tree for all the numbers that are factors of the number on the tree trunk. Write them in the correct pairs. The first one is done for you.

Example

a **20 →**
  2 × 10
  4 × 5

a
10 4
9 11 3
5 2
20

b
3 15
6 5
14
2 10
30

c
10
2 8
20 5
4 17
40

d
7 5
6
3 2 1
8 15
15

e
4 9
5 3
6 2
18

f
4
3
2 8
9
12 5
6
24

g
4 8
6
4 7
10 2
16

h
3
7
4 1 6
3
2 9
9

1 For each set of numbers multiply one number by the other number to find the product.

Example

6 2
?
6 × 2 = 12

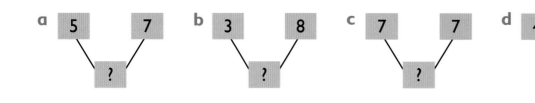

a 5 — 7 ?

b 3 — 8 ?

c 7 — 7 ?

d 4 — 6 ?

106

2 Find the missing factors.

a ? ?   b ? ?   c ? ?   d ? ?

20   15   36   42

3 Build your own factor trees. Use the numbers below to start. What products can be made?

a 2 2 3 2

b 2 3 3 3

c 2 2 2 2

d 3 2 3 2

e 3 5 2 2

f 5 3 3

g 2 2 2 2 3

h 5 3 3

i 3 3 3 3

j 2 2 2 3 2 2

k 5 7 3

l 5 2 7 3

Build your own 5 factor trees.
Choose a number from the apple tree.
Start with the product. Write the pairs of factors.

Example

24
6   4
3 2 2 2

54 36 48 72 28 32 84 63 100 76 24

Using factors to multiply and divide

Use factors to multiply and divide a two-digit number by a one-digit number

Find the factors of these numbers.

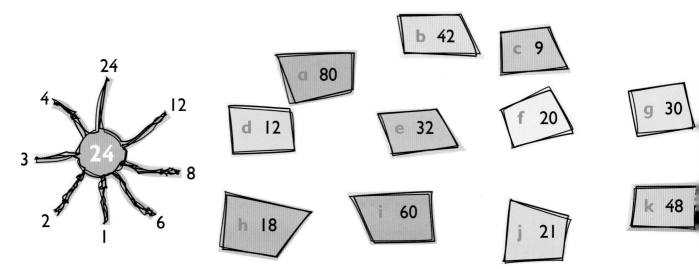

24

4   12

3   **24**   8

2   6

1

a   80

b   42

c   9

d   12

e   32

f   20

g   30

h   18

i   60

j   21

k   48

① Find as many ways as you can to split these calculations using factors to help you.

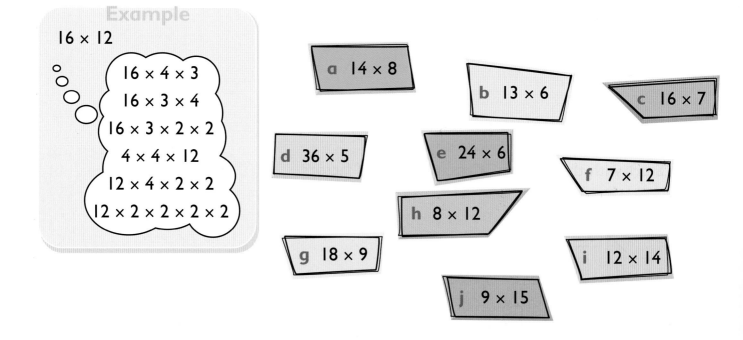

Example

16 × 12

16 × 4 × 3
16 × 3 × 4
16 × 3 × 2 × 2
4 × 4 × 12
12 × 4 × 2 × 2
12 × 2 × 2 × 2 × 2

a   14 × 8

b   13 × 6

c   16 × 7

d   36 × 5

e   24 × 6

f   7 × 12

g   18 × 9

h   8 × 12

i   12 × 14

j   9 × 15

2 a For each of the calculations in question **1**, circle the calculation you made using factors that you find easiest to work out.

b Write the answer to the calculation.

3 Find as many ways as you can to split these calculations using factors to help you.

Example

90 ÷ 6

(90 ÷ 3) ÷ 2
(90 ÷ 2) ÷ 3
(30 ÷ 6) + (30 ÷ 6) + (30 ÷ 6)

a 72 ÷ 6

b 126 ÷ 9

c 76 ÷ 4

d 96 ÷ 8

e 84 ÷ 6

f 56 ÷ 4

4 a For each of the calculations in question **3**, circle the calculation you made using factors that you find easiest to work out.

b Write the answer to the calculation.

Make your own 'two-digit by two-digit' multiplication calculations.
How many different calculations can you make for each number sentence?

Example

5 × 5 × 5 × 3 × 2

→ 25 × 30 (5 × 5) × (5 × 3 × 2)
→ 50 × 15 (5 × 5 × 2) × (5 × 3)
→ 75 × 10 (5 × 5 × 3) × (5 × 2)

a 2 × 2 × 2 × 3 × 3 × 2 × 2

b 2 × 2 × 5 × 3 × 3 × 2

c 2 × 2 × 5 × 3 × 3 × 2

d 3 × 2 × 7 × 3 × 3 × 5

e 3 × 4 × 2 × 2 × 3 × 7 × 2

f 3 × 2 × 4 × 2 × 4 × 2 × 3

Quick 50 and 25

Use known facts and halving to multiply by 50 and 25

1. Multiply the number shown on the calculator display by 100. Write the new number.

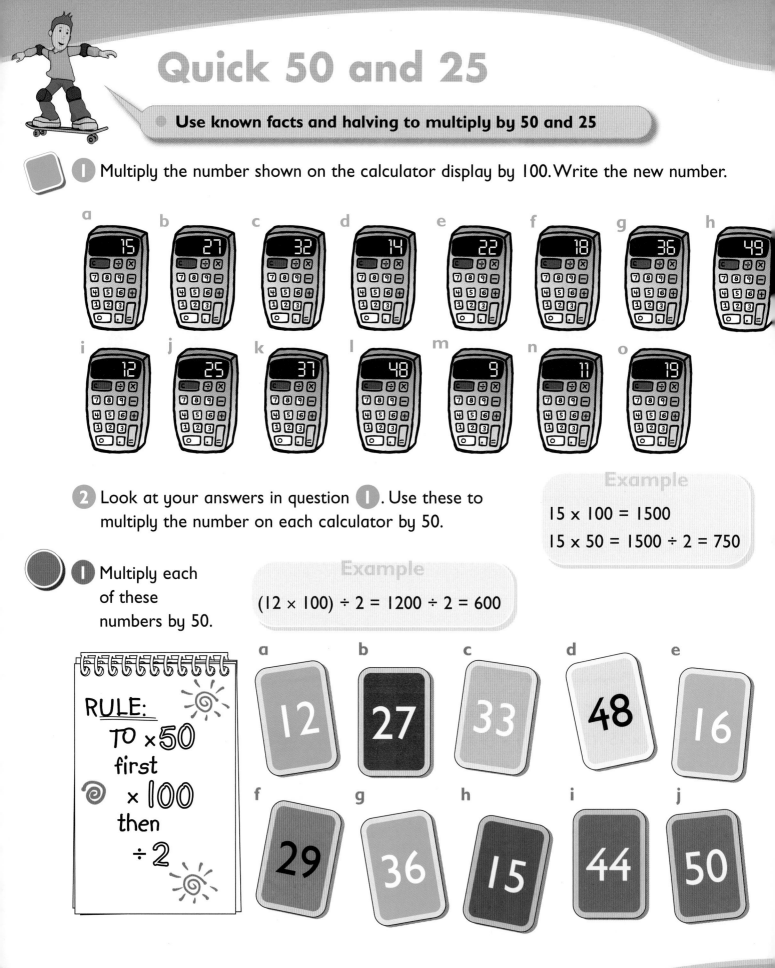

a 15 b 27 c 32 d 14 e 22 f 18 g 36 h 49

i 12 j 25 k 37 l 48 m 9 n 11 o 19

2. Look at your answers in question ①. Use these to multiply the number on each calculator by 50.

Example

15 × 100 = 1500
15 × 50 = 1500 ÷ 2 = 750

① Multiply each of these numbers by 50.

Example

(12 × 100) ÷ 2 = 1200 ÷ 2 = 600

RULE:
To ×50
first
⊙ ×100
then
÷2

a 12 b 27 c 33 d 48 e 16

f 29 g 36 h 15 i 44 j 50

2 Multiply each of these numbers by 25.

RULE:
TO ×25
first
× 100
then ÷ 2
and ÷ 2 again

a **11**
b **14**
c **46**
d **35**
e **22**
f **44**
g **20**
h **17**
i **30**
j **26**

This is a doubling and halving pattern for you to try.
It works when one of the numbers you are multiplying ends in 5.

- Double the number that ends in 5.
- Halve the other number.
- What is the answer?

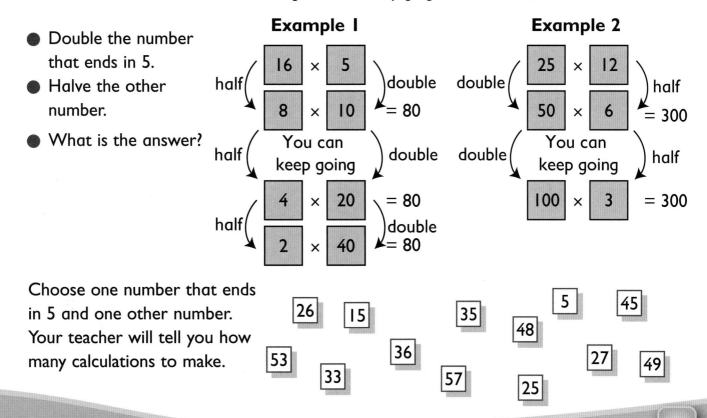

Example 1

half (16 × 5) double
8 × 10 = 80

half (You can keep going) double

4 × 20 = 80
half (2 × 40) double = 80

Example 2

double (25 × 12) half
50 × 6 = 300

double (You can keep going) half

100 × 3 = 300

Choose one number that ends in 5 and one other number. Your teacher will tell you how many calculations to make.

26 15 35 5 45
48
53 36 27 49
33 57 25

Multiplication methods

Multiply a 3-digit number by a one-digit number

1 Multiply each of the numbers in the bag by the number on the label.

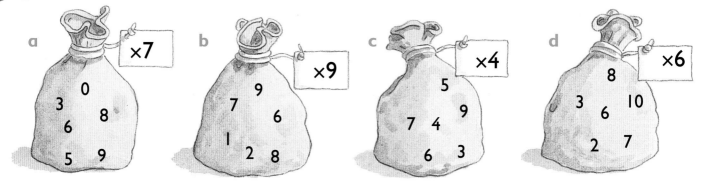

a ×7
0
3 8
6
5 9

b ×9
9
7
6
1
2 8

c ×4
5
9
7 4
6 3

d ×6
8
3 10
6
2 7

2 Partition each of these calculations. The first one has been done for you.

Example

264 × 6 = (200 × 6) + (60 × 6) + (4 × 6)
        = 1200 + 360 + 24
        = 1584

+   200   60   4
6 | 1200 | 360 | 24 | =   1200
                           360
                         + 24
                          1584

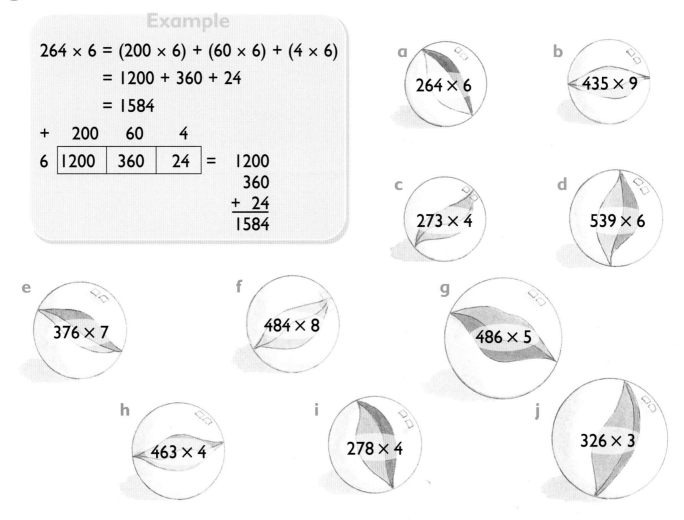

a 264 × 6

b 435 × 9

c 273 × 4

d 539 × 6

e 376 × 7

f 484 × 8

g 486 × 5

h 463 × 4

i 278 × 4

j 326 × 3

Look at the calculations below. Approximate your answer first. Then use an efficient written method to work out the answer to each calculation.

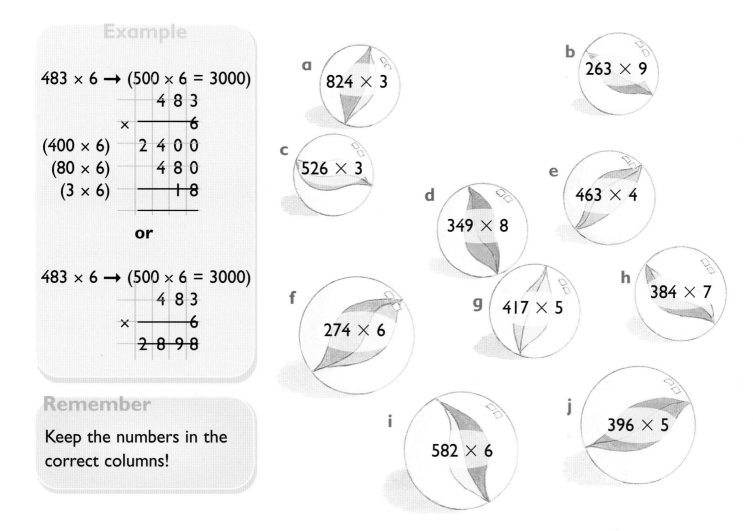

Example

$483 \times 6 \rightarrow (500 \times 6 = 3000)$

$$
\begin{array}{r}
4\ 8\ 3 \\
\times \quad 6 \\
\hline
\end{array}
$$

(400×6) 2 4 0 0
(80×6) 4 8 0
(3×6) 1 8

or

$483 \times 6 \rightarrow (500 \times 6 = 3000)$

$$
\begin{array}{r}
4\ 8\ 3 \\
\times \quad 6 \\
\hline
2\ 8\ 9\ 8
\end{array}
$$

Remember

Keep the numbers in the correct columns!

a 824×3

b 263×9

c 526×3

d 349×8

e 463×4

f 274×6

g 417×5

h 384×7

i 582×6

j 396×5

1. Copy the centre grid.
2. Multiply the numbers on the left by a number on the right.
3. Can you find the correct calculations? Write the calculation in the correct square on the grid.

294
253
469
238
246
337
455

4221	2277	1176
2359	2696	2352
1771	1428	1820

9
7
4
6
8

More multiplication methods

Multiply a pair of two-digit numbers

Copy and complete.
Write the multiples of 10 each number is between.
Circle which multiple of 10 the number is closest to.

Example

70 ← 78 → (80)

a	← 46 →	f	← 54 →	k	← 57 →
b	← 93 →	g	← 61 →	l	← 78 →
c	← 39 →	h	← 17 →	m	← 64 →
d	← 25 →	i	← 33 →	n	← 96 →
e	← 82 →	j	← 85 →	o	← 73 →

1 Approximate the answer to each calculation.

Example

$40 \times 20 = 800$

a 36×19

b 67×31

c 18×45

d 48×72

e 54×63

f 24×32

g 27×35

h 23×58

i 38×28

j 47×48

k 76×68

l 58×46

2 For each of the calculations in question **1**, use the grid method to work out the answer. Match the answer to its calculation.

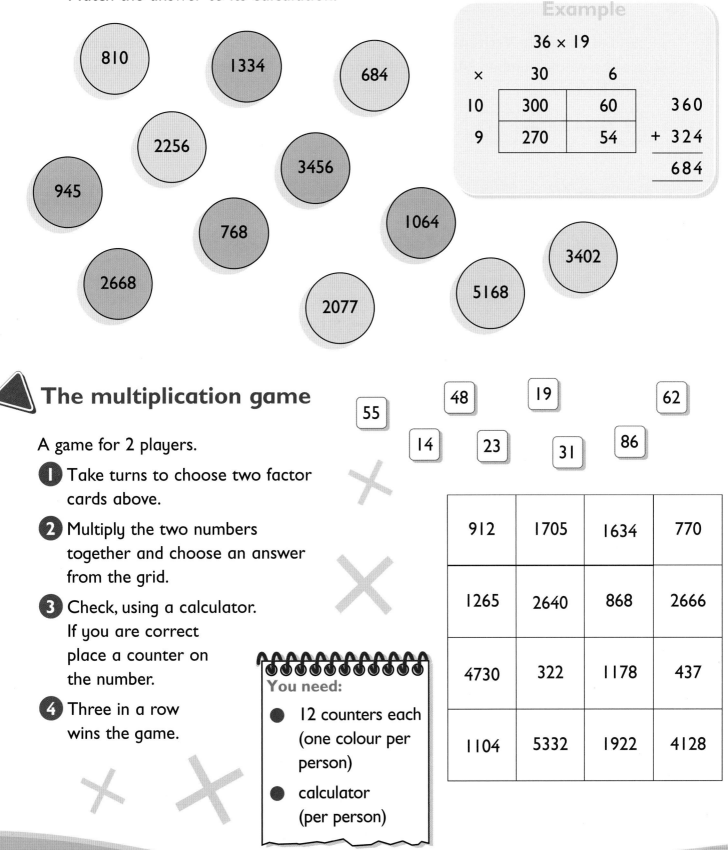

810

1334

684

2256

3456

945

768

1064

2668

3402

2077

5168

Example

36 × 19

×	30	6	
10	300	60	360
9	270	54	+ 324
			684

The multiplication game

A game for 2 players.

1 Take turns to choose two factor cards above.

2 Multiply the two numbers together and choose an answer from the grid.

3 Check, using a calculator. If you are correct place a counter on the number.

4 Three in a row wins the game.

55

48

19

62

14

23

31

86

912	1705	1634	770
1265	2640	868	2666
4730	322	1178	437
1104	5332	1922	4128

You need:

● 12 counters each (one colour per person)

● calculator (per person)

Multiplying decimals

Multiply decimals by a one-digit number

Copy and complete. Write the whole numbers that each decimal number is **between**. Circle the whole number which the decimal number is closest to. The first one is done for you.

a (3) ← 3·4 → 4   b ☐ ← 2·4 → ☐   c ☐ ← 9·7 → ☐

d ☐ ← 4·7 → ☐   e ☐ ← 3·8 → ☐   f ☐ ← 4·0 → ☐

g ☐ ← 8·5 → ☐   h ☐ ← 5·5 → ☐   i ☐ ← 2·9 → ☐

j ☐ ← 9·2 → ☐   k ☐ ← 4·1 → ☐   l ☐ ← 7·3 → ☐

m ☐ ← 1·6 → ☐   n ☐ ← 6·9 → ☐   o ☐ ← 8·2 → ☐

The function machines partition numbers into whole numbers and decimal numbers.

1 Write the number as it will come out of the machine.

Example

6·2 = (6·0 + 0·2)

a

4·3
2·7
6·8
7·5
3·1

b

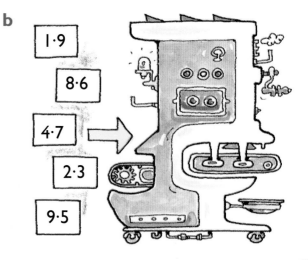

1·9
8·6
4·7
2·3
9·5

116

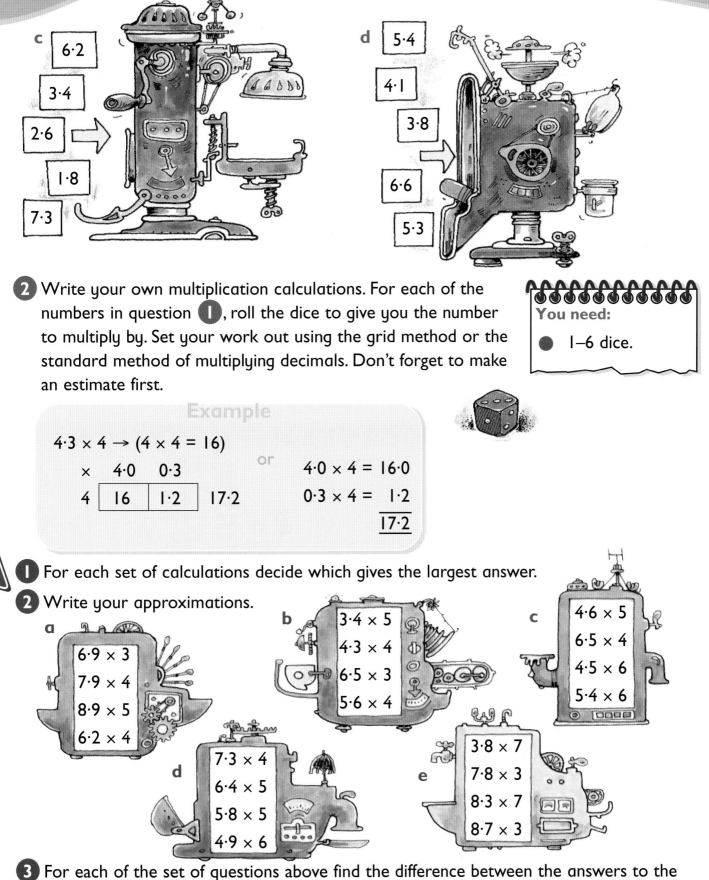

c

6·2

3·4

2·6

1·8

7·3

d

5·4

4·1

3·8

6·6

5·3

2 Write your own multiplication calculations. For each of the numbers in question **1**, roll the dice to give you the number to multiply by. Set your work out using the grid method or the standard method of multiplying decimals. Don't forget to make an estimate first.

You need:

● 1–6 dice.

Example

$4·3 \times 4 \rightarrow (4 \times 4 = 16)$

×	4·0	0·3	
4	16	1·2	17·2

or

$4·0 \times 4 = 16·0$

$0·3 \times 4 = \underline{1·2}$

$\underline{17·2}$

1 For each set of calculations decide which gives the largest answer.

2 Write your approximations.

a

6·9 × 3
7·9 × 4
8·9 × 5
6·2 × 4

b

3·4 × 5
4·3 × 4
6·5 × 3
5·6 × 4

c

4·6 × 5
6·5 × 4
4·5 × 6
5·4 × 6

d

7·3 × 4
6·4 × 5
5·8 × 5
4·9 × 6

e

3·8 × 7
7·8 × 3
8·3 × 7
8·7 × 3

3 For each of the set of questions above find the difference between the answers to the largest and the smallest calculations.

Reviewing multiplication

Refine and use efficient written methods to multiply

Example

$246 \times 7 \to 250 \times 7 = 1750$

×	200	40	6
7	1400	280	42

1400	
280	
+ 42	
1722	
1	

or

246	
× 7	
1400	(200 × 7)
280	(40 × 7)
42	(6 × 7)
1722	
1	

Approximate the answer to each of these calculations, then use a written method to work out the answer.

a 678 × 7

b 538 × 8

c 248 × 5

d 678 × 7

e 463 × 3

f 308 × 9

g 537 × 6

h 449 × 9

i 825 × 4

j 675 × 8

Example

$28 \times 46 \to 30 \times 45 = 1350$

×	20	8
40	800	320
6	120	48

800	
320	
120	
+ 48	
1288	

or

28	
× 46	
1120	(40 × 28)
168	(6 × 28)
1288	

1 Approximate the answer to each of these calculations, then use a written method to work out the answer.

a 78 × 68

b 57 × 72

c 86 × 82

d 28 × 45

e 67 × 93

f 49 × 56

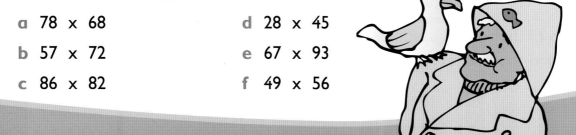

118

Example

$$5{\cdot}3 \times 8 \rightarrow 5 \times 8 = 40$$

×	5·0	0·3
8	40	2·4

```
   40
+   2·4
  ────
  42·4
```

or

```
   5·3
 ×   8
 ─────
   40    (5·0 × 8)
    2·4  (0·3 × 8)
  ─────
  42·4
```

2 Approximate the answer to each of these calculations, then use a written method to work out the answer.

a 5·8 × 6   d 6·7 × 4

b 9·5 × 7   e 4·3 × 5

c 7·8 × 9   f 8·6 × 8

Estimating products

A game for 2 players.

| 865 | 34 | 8·3 | 74 | 9·6 | 494 |

| 639 | 4·9 | 93 | 748 | 6·5 | 47 |

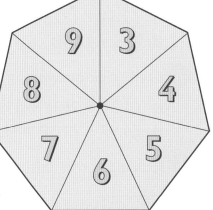

- One player places a counter on one of the flags.

- The other player spins the spinner.

- Each player writes down an estimate of the product of these two numbers.

- Each player then calculates the answer and checks to see if they both have the same answer.

- The winner is the player with the smaller difference between their estimate and the actual answer.

- Play 10 rounds. The overall winner is the player who wins more rounds.

You need:
- counter
- paper clip
- pencil and paper each

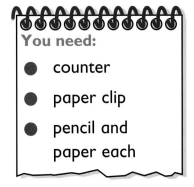

Money calculations

Develop calculator skills and use a calculator effectively

Work out these calculations, giving your answers in pounds and pence.

You need:
- calculator

a 90p + 47p

b 265p – 99p

c 348p ÷ 4

d 9 x 57p

e 150p + 70p

f 320p – 245p

g 410p ÷ 5

h 6 x 15p

i £1.56 + £3.47

j £9.26 – £3.57

k £10.76 + £13.85

l £2.43 x 8

m £6.57 x 9

n £6.02 ÷ 7

o £5.08 ÷ 4

p £13.25 – £9.76

q £13.67 + £8.52

r £12.74 – £9.77

1 Calculate the answers in pence. Change pounds to pence first.

You need:
- calculator

a 72p + £1.84

b 60p + £4.48

c £2.20 + 151p

d £2.25 + 95p

e £5.63 + 117p

f 8p + £8.96

2 Convert your answers to question **1** to pounds and pence.

3 Calculate these answers in pounds and pence. Change pence to pounds first.

a £3.44 + 172p

b £2.50 + 465p

c £1.56 + 71p

d 49p + £6.98

e 87p + £3.23

f 40p + £12.70

4 Give your answers in pounds and pence.

a £1.34 + 263p + 159p

b 152p + £7.10 + £2.28

c 75p + £1.20 + 86p

d £4.99 + £1.50 + 66p

e £1.25 + 29p + £3.21 + 48p

f 6p + £4.16 + £1.21 + £7

5 Calculate the difference in price.

a

£3.34   198p

b

76p   £2.51

c

95p   £2.25

d

£3   84p

6 Nancy saves 85p every week. How much does she save in:

a 5 weeks　　　　　　b 12 weeks　　　　　　c 40 weeks?

Give your answers in pounds and pence.

7 Four children saved the same amount of money every week.
How much did they save each week?

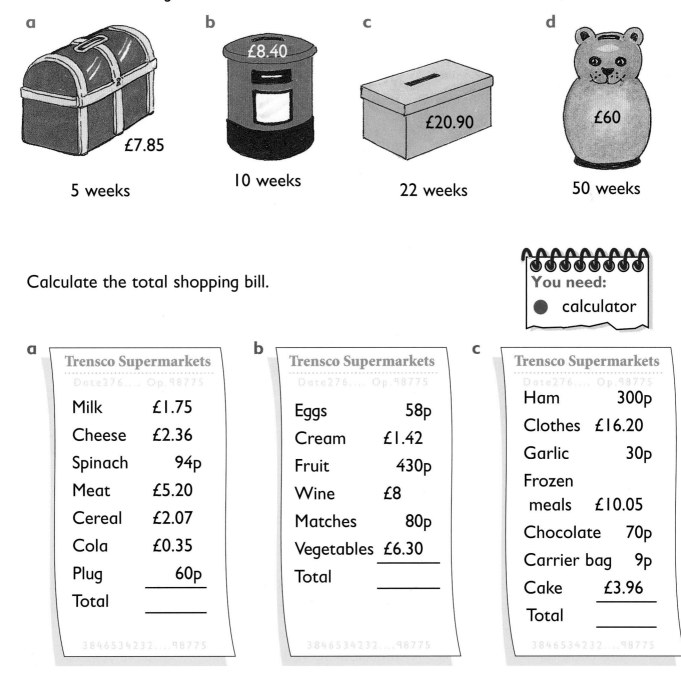

a
£7.85
5 weeks

b
£8.40
10 weeks

c
£20.90
22 weeks

d
£60
50 weeks

Calculate the total shopping bill.

You need:
● calculator

a

Trensco Supermarkets

Date276.... Op.98775

Milk	£1.75
Cheese	£2.36
Spinach	94p
Meat	£5.20
Cereal	£2.07
Cola	£0.35
Plug	60p
Total	

3846534232....98775

b

Trensco Supermarkets

Date276.... Op.98775

Eggs	58p
Cream	£1.42
Fruit	430p
Wine	£8
Matches	80p
Vegetables	£6.30
Total	

3846534232....98775

c

Trensco Supermarkets

Date276.... Op.98775

Ham	300p
Clothes	£16.20
Garlic	30p
Frozen meals	£10.05
Chocolate	70p
Carrier bag	9p
Cake	£3.96
Total	

3846534232....98775

Solving word problems

● **Solve one- and two-step problems**

Read the word problems. Choose an appropriate method of calculating your answer:
● Mental   ● Mental with jottings   ● Pencil and paper

Show all your working.

a On one day, 124 people each paid £4 to go on the Ghost Train at a fair. How much money did the Ghost train make in a day?

b At an airport, Rav buys a puzzle book for £3.75, a drink for £1.10 and a magazine for £2.40. How much did Rav spend altogether?

c Sam has read 85 pages of the 264 pages in his book. How many more pages must he read to finish the book?

d A plane can carry 245 passengers. 62 of the seats are empty. How many passengers are on the plane?

e A car park has 14 equal rows. Each row can hold 20 cars. How many cars can the car park hold?

f There are 200 paper clips in a box. How many paper clips are there in 8 boxes?

g 436 people visited a park on Saturday. On Sunday there were 122 more visitors to the park. How many people visited the park on Sunday?

h A box holds 72 eggs arranged in cartons, each carton containing 6 eggs. How many cartons are there in the box?

i There are 573 children in a school. 271 of them are boys. How many girls are in the school?

Read the word problems. Choose an appropriate method of calculating your answer:
● Mental   ● Mental with jottings   ● Pencil and paper

Show all your working.

a Louise has read 97 pages of a 228 page book. How many more pages must she read to reach the middle of the book?

b A can of soup weighs 320 g. Three cans of soup are cooked and equal amounts served into 5 bowls. How many grams of soup are there in each bowl?

c An omelette uses 2 eggs. Eggs costs £1.50 for 6. How much does it cost to make 4 omelettes?

d A round trip on the number 42 bus is 34 km. Dave, the number 42 bus driver, does the round trip 3 times a day, 5 days a week. How many kilometres is this in a week?

e Tom is 82 years old. His son Paul is 46 years younger than Tom. Paul's daughter Samantha is 29 years younger than Paul. How old is Samantha?

f There are 20 toffees in a box. Josh eats $\frac{2}{5}$ of them. Derek eats $\frac{1}{5}$ of them. How many chocolates are left?

g Brian is saving to buy a new computer costing £862. He has already saved £509. His mother gives him another £150. How much more does Brain need to save?

h Strawberry lollies cost 85p each and Ice Wonders cost 62p each. Jane buys 4 Strawberry lollies and 3 Ice Wonders. How much does she spend altogether?

i Sam buys 5 cans of lemonade, each containing 330 ml. He gives the shopkeeper £10 and gets £6 change. How much does 1 can of lemonade cost?

Would you be willing to take just one penny as pocket money this week, as long as each week after that the amount of money would double?

How much pocket money would you get in the 8th week?

What about the 12th week? 15th week? 20th week? 24th week?

Maths Facts

The seven steps to problem solving

1 Read the problem carefully. **2** What do you have to find?

3 What facts are given? **4** Which of the facts do you need?

5 Make a plan. **6** Carry out your plan to obtain your answer. **7** Check your answer.

Number

Positive and negative numbers

$$-10 \quad -9 \quad -8 \quad -7 \quad -6 \quad -5 \quad -4 \quad -3 \quad -2 \quad -1 \quad 0 \quad 1 \quad 2 \quad 3 \quad 4 \quad 5 \quad 6 \quad 7 \quad 8 \quad 9 \quad 10$$

Place value

1000	2000	3000	4000	5000	6000	7000	8000	9000
100	200	300	400	500	600	700	800	900
10	20	30	40	50	60	70	80	90
1	2	3	4	5	6	7	8	9
0·1	0·2	0·3	0·4	0·5	0·6	0·7	0·8	0·9
0·01	0·02	0·03	0·04	0·05	0·06	0·07	0·08	0·09
0·001	0·002	0·003	0·004	0·005	0·006	0·007	0·008	0·009

Fractions, decimals and percentages

$\frac{1}{100} = 0 \cdot 01 = 1\%$ $\frac{2}{100} = \frac{1}{50} = 0 \cdot 02 = 2\%$ $\frac{5}{100} = \frac{1}{20} = 0 \cdot 05 = 5\%$

$\frac{10}{100} = \frac{1}{10} = 0 \cdot 1 = 10\%$ $\frac{1}{8} = 0 \cdot 125 = 12 \cdot 5\%$ $\frac{20}{100} = \frac{1}{5} = 0 \cdot 2 = 20\%$

$\frac{25}{100} = \frac{1}{4} = 0 \cdot 25 = 25\%$ $\frac{1}{3} = 0 \cdot 333 = 33\frac{1}{3}\%$ $\frac{50}{100} = \frac{1}{2} = 0 \cdot 5 = 50\%$

$\frac{2}{3} = 0 \cdot 667 = 66\frac{2}{3}\%$ $\frac{75}{100} = \frac{3}{4} = 0 \cdot 75 = 75\%$ $\frac{100}{100} = 1 = 100\%$

Number facts

Multiplication and division facts

	×1	×2	×3	×4	×5	×6	×7	×8	×9	×10
×1	1	2	3	4	5	6	7	8	9	10
×2	2	4	6	8	10	12	14	16	18	20
×3	3	6	9	12	15	18	21	24	27	30
×4	4	8	12	16	20	24	28	32	36	40
×5	5	10	15	20	25	30	35	40	45	50
×6	6	12	18	24	30	36	42	48	54	60
×7	7	14	21	28	35	42	49	56	63	70
×8	8	16	24	32	40	48	56	64	72	80
×9	9	18	27	36	45	54	63	72	81	90
×10	10	20	30	40	50	60	70	80	90	100

Tests of divisibility

2 The last digit is 0, 2, 4, 6 or 8.

3 The sum of the digits is divisible by 3.

4 The last two digits are divisible by 4.

5 The last digit is 5 or 0.

6 It is divisible by both 2 and 3.

7 Check a known near multiple of 7.

8 Half of it is divisible by 4 *or*
The last 3 digits are divisible by 8.

9 The sum of the digits is divisible by 9.

10 The last digit is 0.

Calculations

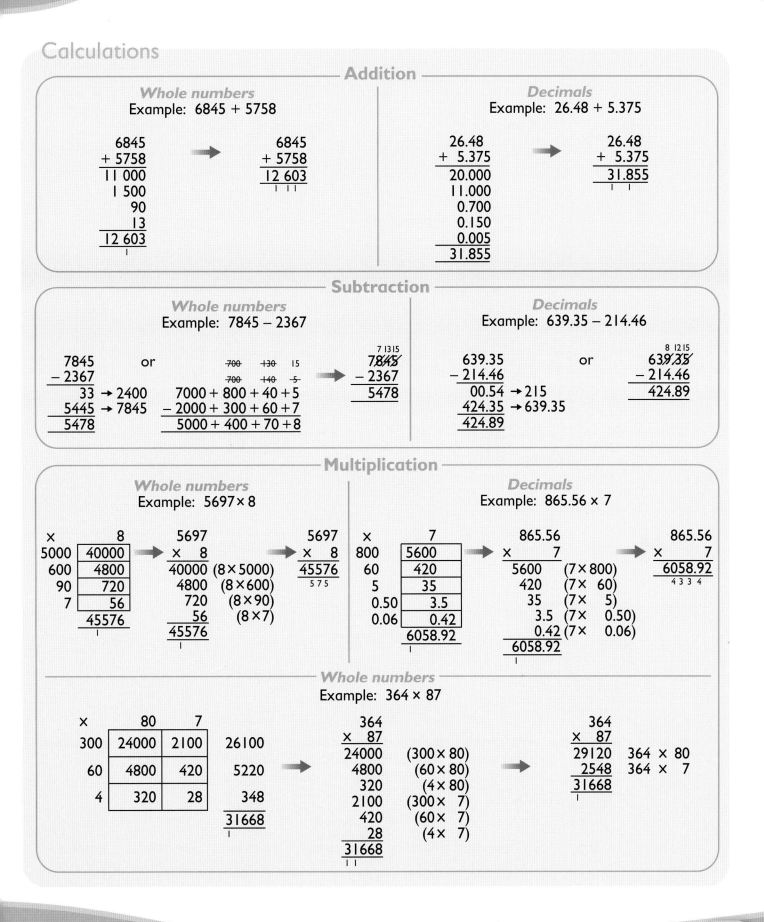

Addition

Whole numbers
Example: 6845 + 5758

```
    6845              6845
  + 5758            + 5758
  11 000            12 603
   1 500              1 1 1
     90
     13
  12 603
      1
```

Decimals
Example: 26.48 + 5.375

```
    26.48             26.48
  +  5.375          +  5.375
   20.000           31.855
   11.000            1 1
    0.700
    0.150
    0.005
   31.855
```

Subtraction

Whole numbers
Example: 7845 − 2367

```
  7845    or                                     7 13 15
− 2367              700    +30    15             7 8 4 5
   33 → 2400        700    +40    −5           − 2367
 5445 → 7845     7000 + 800 + 40 + 5             5478
 5478            − 2000 + 300 + 60 + 7
                 5000 + 400 + 70 + 8
```

Decimals
Example: 639.35 − 214.46

```
  639.35     or                    8 12 15
− 214.46                          6 3 9. 3 5
   00.54 → 215                  − 214.46
  424.35 → 639.35                 424.89
  424.89
```

Multiplication

Whole numbers
Example: 5697 × 8

```
  ×        8          5697               5697
5000 │ 40000 │     ×     8            ×     8
 600 │  4800 │     40000 (8×5000)       45576
  90 │   720 │      4800 (8×600)         5 7 5
   7 │    56 │       720 (8×90)
       45576           56 (8×7)
           1        45576
                        1
```

Decimals
Example: 865.56 × 7

```
   ×        7          865.56              865.56
 800 │  5600 │      ×      7            ×      7
  60 │   420 │       5600 (7×800)         6058.92
   5 │    35 │        420 (7×60)           4 3 3 4
0.50 │   3.5 │         35 (7×5)
0.06 │  0.42 │        3.5 (7×0.50)
       6058.92        0.42 (7×0.06)
           1        6058.92
                        1
```

Whole numbers
Example: 364 × 87

```
  ×      80      7
300 │ 24000 │ 2100 │   26100
 60 │  4800 │  420 │    5220
  4 │   320 │   28 │     348
                       31668
                           1
```

```
    364
  ×  87
  24000   (300×80)
   4800   (60×80)
    320   (4×80)
   2100   (300×7)
    420   (60×7)
     28   (4×7)
  31668
    1 1
```

```
    364
  ×  87
  29120   364 × 80
   2548   364 × 7
  31668
      1
```

Calculations

Division

Whole numbers
Example: 337 ÷ 8

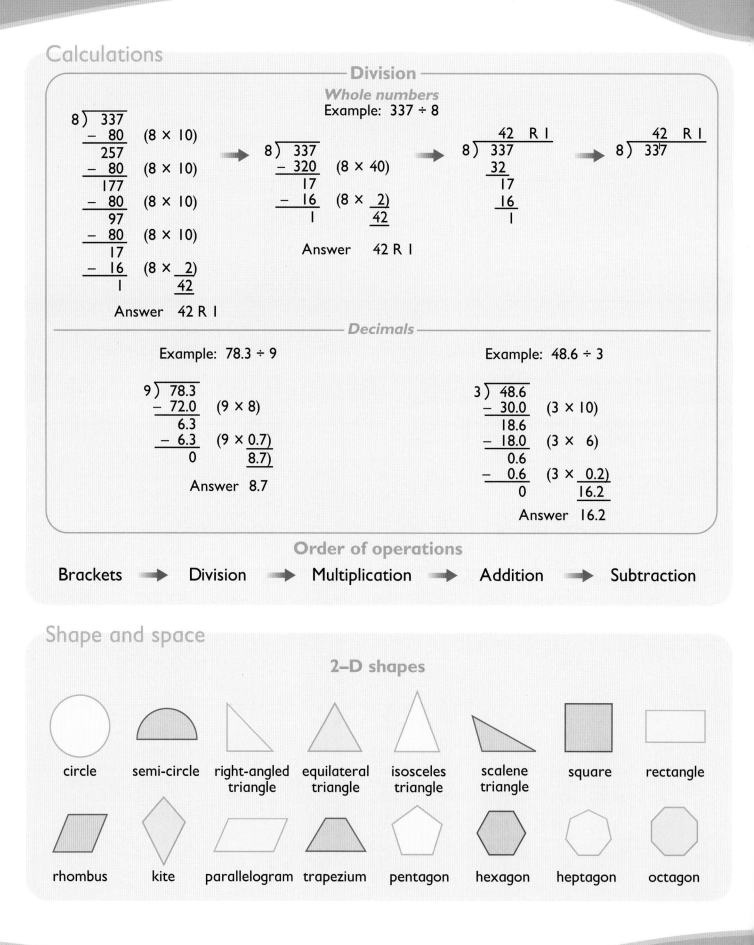

```
8) 337
  - 80    (8 × 10)
   257
  - 80    (8 × 10)
   177
  - 80    (8 × 10)
    97
  - 80    (8 × 10)
    17
  - 16    (8 ×  2)
     1         42
```
Answer   42 R 1

```
8) 337
  - 320    (8 × 40)
    17
  - 16     (8 ×  2)
     1          42
```
Answer   42 R 1

```
    42   R 1
8) 337
   32
   17
   16
    1
```

```
    42   R 1
8) 337
```

Decimals

Example: 78.3 ÷ 9

```
9) 78.3
  - 72.0    (9 × 8)
    6.3
  - 6.3     (9 × 0.7)
    0            8.7)
```
Answer 8.7

Example: 48.6 ÷ 3

```
3) 48.6
  - 30.0    (3 × 10)
   18.6
  - 18.0    (3 ×  6)
    0.6
  - 0.6     (3 × 0.2)
    0           16.2
```
Answer 16.2

Order of operations

Brackets → Division → Multiplication → Addition → Subtraction

Shape and space

2–D shapes

circle   semi-circle   right-angled triangle   equilateral triangle   isosceles triangle   scalene triangle   square   rectangle

rhombus   kite   parallelogram   trapezium   pentagon   hexagon   heptagon   octagon

Shape and space

3–D solids

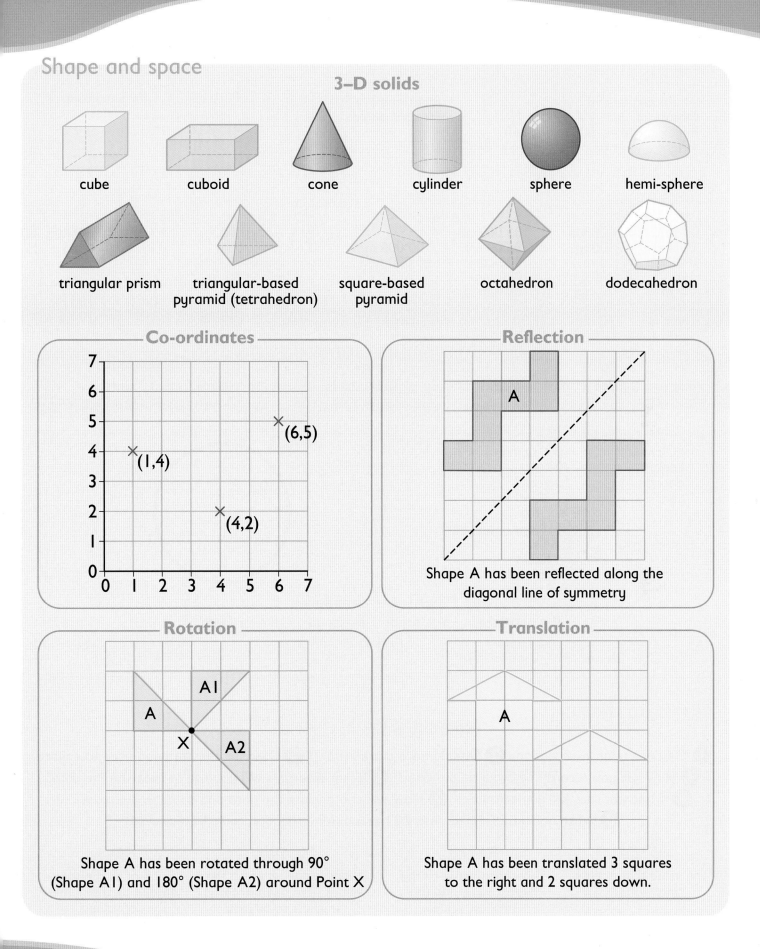

cube   cuboid   cone   cylinder   sphere   hemi-sphere

triangular prism   triangular-based pyramid (tetrahedron)   square-based pyramid   octahedron   dodecahedron

Co-ordinates

(1,4)   (6,5)   (4,2)

Reflection

Shape A has been reflected along the diagonal line of symmetry

Rotation

Shape A has been rotated through 90° (Shape A1) and 180° (Shape A2) around Point X

Translation

Shape A has been translated 3 squares to the right and 2 squares down.

Shape and space

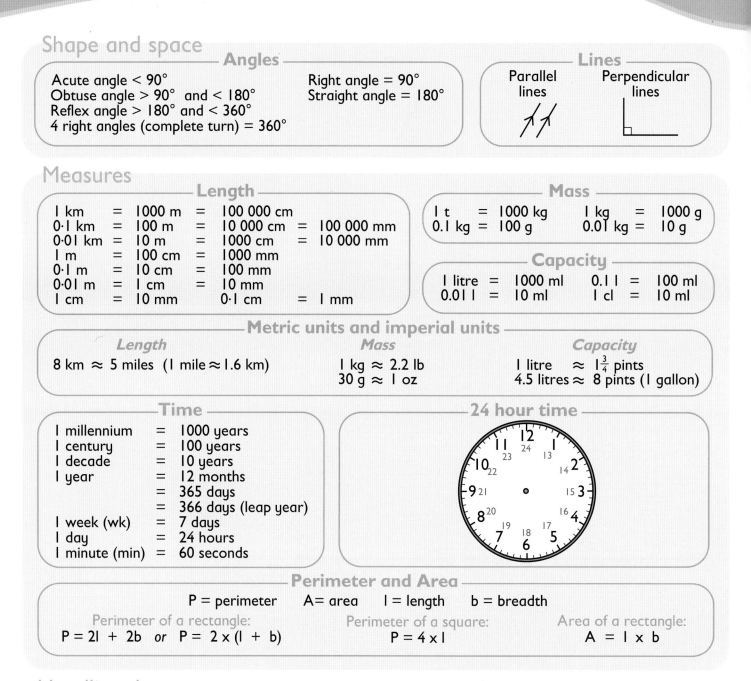

Angles

Acute angle < 90°
Obtuse angle > 90° and < 180°
Reflex angle > 180° and < 360°
4 right angles (complete turn) = 360°

Right angle = 90°
Straight angle = 180°

Lines

Parallel lines

Perpendicular lines

Measures

Length

I km	= 1000 m	= 100 000 cm		
0·1 km	= 100 m	= 10 000 cm	= 100 000 mm	
0·01 km	= 10 m	= 1000 cm	= 10 000 mm	
I m	= 100 cm	= 1000 mm		
0·1 m	= 10 cm	= 100 mm		
0·01 m	= 1 cm	= 10 mm		
I cm	= 10 mm	0·1 cm	= 1 mm	

Mass

I t	= 1000 kg	I kg	= 1000 g
0.1 kg	= 100 g	0.01 kg	= 10 g

Capacity

I litre	= 1000 ml	0.1 l	= 100 ml
0.01 l	= 10 ml	I cl	= 10 ml

Metric units and imperial units

Length
8 km ≈ 5 miles (1 mile ≈ 1.6 km)

Mass
I kg ≈ 2.2 lb
30 g ≈ 1 oz

Capacity
I litre ≈ $1\frac{3}{4}$ pints
4.5 litres ≈ 8 pints (1 gallon)

Time

I millennium	=	1000 years
I century	=	100 years
I decade	=	10 years
I year	=	12 months
	=	365 days
	=	366 days (leap year)
I week (wk)	=	7 days
I day	=	24 hours
I minute (min)	=	60 seconds

24 hour time

Perimeter and Area

P = perimeter   A = area   l = length   b = breadth

Perimeter of a rectangle:
P = 2l + 2b *or* P = 2 x (l + b)

Perimeter of a square:
P = 4 x l

Area of a rectangle:
A = l x b

Handling data

Planning an investigation

1 Describe your investigation. **2** Do you have a prediction? **3** Describe the data you need to collect. **4** How will you record and organise the data? **5** What diagrams will you use to illustrate the data? **6** What statistics will you calculate? **7** How will you analyse the data and come to a conclusion? **8** When you have finished, describe how your investigation could be improved.

Mode
The value that occurs most often.

Range
Difference between the largest value and the smallest value.

Median
Middle value when all the values have been ordered smallest to largest.

Mean
Total of all the values divided by the number of values.